The HUNTERS and the HUNTED

Karl and Kathrine
Ammann

The
HUNTERS
and the
HUNTED

Camerapix Publishers International

NAIROBI

First published 1989 by
Camerapix,
P.O. Box 45048,
Nairobi, Kenya

© K & K Ammann, Camerapix 1989

A CIP Catalogue record for this book
is available from the British Library.

ISBN 0 370 31239 2

This book was designed and produced by
Camerapix Publishers International,
P.O. Box 45048,
Nairobi, Kenya

Edited by Brian Tetley
Typeset by Nazma Rawji and Barbara Lawrence
Design: Craig Dodd

Printed by Mandarin Offset, Hong Kong

Title: Impala in flight in the Mara.

Contents

Introduction

Under African Skies
by Ian Parker

Africa is a panoramic land of rolling, golden plains and far blue mountain ranges. With its teeming wildlife it creates a sense of permanence, a feeling that it must have been so from the dawn of life. Striking ancient chords deep in the subconscious, perhaps stirring a recognition that *this* is man's ancestral home, where it all began, Africa seems timeless and changeless.

The feeling is illusory. Africa's past is as varied as that of any other continent. Up to twelve million years ago — a mere eye blink in geological terms — the continent was largely flat and low-lying. But the movements of the earth's crust changed this. The great continental plates have never been still. Rising up and sinking into the planet's molten magma, they caused Africa to warp and buckle. Arching its back, immense blocks were lifted into high plateaux.

Molten fingers probed the new crust, seeking fractures and weaknesses to exploit. Volcanic pressures below blasted fiery materials skywards in huge explosions. Streams of lava flowed slowly across the land, and plumes of ash and steam drifted into the atmosphere to fall as dry rain in distant places, colouring sunrise and sunset in dramatic hues for decades after. Part of this metamorphosis in old, flat, Africa was the vast crack that split the continent from north to south: the Great Rift Valley.

These geological changes affected Africa's wildlife dramatically. Creatures, including The Hunters and The Hunted, had to adapt to new habitats. More species evolved to colonize and exploit the ecological niches that appeared. Once continuous and extensive ranges were broken up, animals and plants were isolated; developing independently and in different directions to suit local conditions. This Pleiocene and Pleistocene process of rapid geological and ecological change continues. To a great degree it has created the wide and beautiful variety of landscapes, flowers, plants, trees and wildlife that exist in Africa today.

In East Africa the Rift Valley developed two branches: in the west along the border between Uganda and Zaire, and in the east splitting Kenya and Tanzania from north to south. The two meet near Lake Rukwa in the south. Cradled between the Rift's two arms, Uganda, western Kenya and north-western Tanzania form a large upland table. Lake Victoria, the world's second-largest inland sea, lies at the centre of this fertile, well-watered region nurturing man, beast and plant alike. It has become one of Africa's most densely peopled areas.

Yet, between Lake Victoria's south-eastern shores and the eastern Rift, in the Serengeti-Mara ecosystem, there is a wilderness where few people live. Instead, teeming wildlife dominates the grassland plains: more than two million large herbivores — and living off them an array of predators, scavengers and parasites without visual equal.

This wild pageant shows how life has responded to the changes that gave Africa its present shape and appearance. It has some old components, but much that is new and dynamic: an

Opposite: Elephant enjoys the shade of an acacia tree during noonday heat.

Previous pages: Topi silhouetted at sunset.

Following Pages: Zebra stallions in a tussle.

exposition of contemporary evolution. What you now see may be different to anything visible in time gone by and at its most spectacular.

Talk of this ecosystem slips off the tongue a shade too easily. It suggests something finite — a self-contained unit with clear-cut boundaries. Yet the Serengeti-Mara 'system' is man-made, as much a political as biological entity. Its eastern edge is the Rift wall plunging precipitously 2,000 metres from the fringing Loita and Loliondo highlands to the valley below.

In many aspects the plants and animals of the arid, hot floor of the Rift are different to those on the cool heights. Other than the clear streams that cascade into the valley, there is no great interchange between the two. Yet, rising 2,700 metres (8,858 feet) out of the valley is an active ash volcano, the eerie grey cone of Ol Doinyo Lengai — the Maasai's Mountain of God.

Every eight years or so it spews out a dense cloud of pale grey ash which, carried westward by the prevailing winds, falls gently across the southern Serengeti plains. Thus the Serengeti soils are dominated by Ol Doinyo Lengai, miles away to the east in the Rift Valley, exerting so much influence that it cannot be excluded from the ecosystem. The Rift wall is clearly no hard and fast border.

Even less evident are any real boundaries to the north and south. Only in the west, on the lake shore, is any division clearly defined. But even so, rivers and erosion carry Serengeti-Mara soils into the lake and insects and birds return at least some of these elements to the land.

As a conservation area the Serengeti-Mara's roots were planted early this century when adventuring white men laid eyes on the rolling grasslands of Maasailand in south-western Kenya and north-western Tanzania. They beheld plains animals in tens of thousands: wildebeest, gazelle, hartebeest, impala, zebra and others. To their eyes the setting gave a glimpse of untrammelled nature; of a veritable Eden. Inevitably, they wanted to preserve it.

The first concrete steps were taken in Tanganyika, now Tanzania, soon after the First World War, when the Government declared the southern part of the Serengeti a game reserve, proclaiming this, and the Ngorongoro Crater, a national park in 1940. It was thought then that the animals moved seasonally between the Crater and the shores of Lake Victoria. But it soon became apparent that these boundaries, after all, did not cover the seasonal migrations. And so the Serengeti National Park was disconnected from neighbouring Ngorongoro — which became a special conservation area — and pushed northward to the Kenya-Tanzania border.

In Kenya, the Maasai were unwilling to surrender land for a national park. Nevertheless, on the advice of the District Game Warden, Major Lyn Temple-Boreham, they did agree to create their own game reserve. Covering several hundred square kilometres, it was, in effect, an extension of Serengeti National Park. It was proclaimed the Maasai Mara Game Reserve.

The concept of the Serengeti-Mara 'ecosystem', however, is stretched, according to individual scientific whim and inclination, to any land beyond their boundaries that they feel important. And the dynamic aspect of change that is its constant feature has substantially weakened the theory of a well-defined, stable ecosystem. The early idea that the Serengeti-Mara represented nature undisturbed was wrong.

Nobody knows for certain how things were in the distant past. But as hunter and gatherer, man has probably long influenced the region's plants and animals, perhaps initially through starting occasional fires. Later, about six thousand years ago, pastoralists arrived bringing cattle and goats to compete with the wildlife. Where they could, they managed the vegetation to favour grasses. Their regular burning and grazing routines suited open landscapes, to the advantage of the wild grazing species and the disadvantage of the browsers.

From tribal lore there is an indication of what went on in the Serengeti-Mara in the last century. The presence of the Maasai and their cattle, who used most of it and considered it part of their territory, suggests that much of the area must have been open. The numbers of browsing wildlife would probably have been relatively low, and grazers, like wildebeest, thicker on the ground. Competing cattle, sheep, goats and donkeys would have put a brake on their numbers but, even so, it is likely that large wild animals were present in considerable numbers.

A century ago two virulent cattle plagues swept Maasailand: bovine pleuropneumonia and rinderpest. As their herds were decimated, the Maasai fell on hard times. Many cattle died and the people pulled back toward the tribal heartlands, leaving peripheral ranges such as the Serengeti-Mara largely empty. The rinderpest also took its toll of wildebeest and buffalo.

Soon there were only a few people and animals left on the open plains. Trees and bushes invaded the grasslands and the balance swung in favour of browsers. Among the animals and thicket and woodland, the tsetse fly flourished. It carried sleeping sickness, *trypanasomiasis*: a disease fatal to domestic animals and, in some forms, to man.

The tsetse effectively closed much of the area to cattle. Only the dry, southern Serengeti short-grass plains, where soil conditions prevent tree growth, and the land more than 1,500 metres (5,000 feet) high, where it is too cold for them, remained open for livestock.

So it was when the first white men arrived and found this empty land, even though it was known locally as Maasailand.

Like the Maasai cattle, the wildebeest slowly recovered from the initial rinderpest epidemic. It was noted that every year, however, most wildebeest between six months and one year old

Following pages: The Maasai and their livestock — an integral part of the Serengeti-Mara ecosystem.

contracted a sickness which killed large numbers. Known as 'yearlings' disease', it was in fact a mild form of rinderpest. Those which survived became immune. So, too, did the calves — for, while still suckling, they acquired temporary immunity from their mothers. This wore off just after weaning at six months — hence the timing of the annual outbreaks.

Eventually, a rinderpest vaccine for cattle was developed and as soon as the Maasai stock was vaccinated 'yearlings' disease' vanished, removing from the wildebeest a major source of mortality. Their numbers began to increase dramatically.

All about the Serengeti-Mara, at the same time, people and their stock were also increasing, pushing elephant herds towards the conservation areas. Elephants probably also increased during the first half of the century, recovering from losses inflicted by ivory hunting in the nineteenth century. Concentrated in larger numbers, they began to take their toll on the woodlands and thickets. Breaking down the trees and bushes, the elephants allowed grasses, previously shaded out, to flourish. And each season when the grasses dried out, fires lit by lightning, hunters, graziers, game wardens and tourists licked through the thickets, killing many trees and shrubs. The woodlands began to thin out into open grassland. And as they vanished so did the tsetse, dependent on their shade.

In the thirty years and more since 1955 change has spread deep into the Serengeti – Mara. Little real woodland or thicket now remains. As these wildlife conservation areas were closed to domestic stock the wild grazers benefitted without competition. Free of 'yearlings' disease', and with a rapidly-expanding food supply, wildebeest herds rose from around 250,000 in the late 1950s to some 1.4 million in the 1980s.

Other big changes appear to have taken place, too. Earlier, two migrations seemed to occur in the Serengeti-Mara ecosystem. In the dry season, animals ranged near the Mara river — to the north of the present reserve. When the rains broke in Kenya, they moved eastwards onto the dry Loita plains, staying there as long as the water lasted, before drifting west again as the country dried out.

Away to the south, in the southern half of the Serengeti, separated from the Mara by a broad band of woodland, a second, far more pronounced migration occurred. The grazers spent the dry season in areas of permanent water towards Lake Victoria, migrating eastward onto the short-grass plains in and about the southern Serengeti during the wet season.

Steadily, the growing populations of people and livestock curtailed the wet season movements of the Mara animals. And the same happened in the west of the Serengeti, turning the animal migrations more and more to the north. The trend was spurred by the spread of the grasslands as the woods retreated under the impact of elephant and fire.

The loose and semi-independent systems of thirty years ago became integrated. But when the rains fall, thousands of wildebeest still make a westward pass towards Lake Victoria as they move off the southerly short-grass plains. Overwhelmingly, however, the seasonal migration now moves up and down a north-south axis.

In the dry season between July and November the grazers — more than 1.4 million wildebeest, 240,000 gazelles and 200,000 zebra — crowd into the Mara. When the rains break they head rapidly for the short-grasslands some two hundred kilometres to the south and stay there as long as the water pans hold out. There, the wildebeest calve. In the three-week birthing season, the plains are freckled with the bleating, dun-coloured offspring. Indeed, so many are there, that losing mother in the crowd is a major source of calf mortality, for each female will suckle her calf — and her calf only. The youngster that becomes separated is doomed.

As the southern country dries out, the migrants follow the better rainfall to arrive back in the Mara in early July, a spectacle best seen, heard and smelt in the vast theatre of the plains beneath the towering clouds. Experienced alone and on foot, this spectacle puts puny man in true perspective. Surely the tumultuous tide of wildlife surging up and down the Serengeti-Mara each year is one of nature's greatest spectacles, substantially greater in the 1980s than thirty years ago. And man has played a major role in staging it. As no other example, it illustrates man's influence on Africa's evolution. Many modifications to nature may seem undesirable, but this one must surely be positive. If the Serengeti-Mara is a latter-day Eden, then man has been one of its gardeners.

High above the Mara's rolling grasslands, a dove draws a swift line across an azure sky. Higher still, unseen, a peregrine lurks on scimitar wings. Computing interception at a point yet far ahead of the dove, it furls pinions and dips down. Carving an arc down the sky in awesome swoop, the two courses converge with breathtaking speed, precision and symmetry, culminating when the dove is sundered by the falcon's talons.

A brief scuffle disturbs a dappled shade, subsiding in the last protesting kicks from a young impala. The leopard's baleful orbs hold the watcher briefly before it slips arrogantly away. Young wart hogs cavort and whirl in harmless mischief, heedless of life's seriousness. Suddenly — a tawny flash from the background — a lioness erupts onto centre stage. The hoglets are gone. All but one, that is, limp and crushed in the big cat's maw. And we are fascinated.

It's something of a paradox that those who turn to nature for reassurance and inspiration become mesmerized by the discordant excitement of hunting.

Such moments, when one life takes another, leave lasting impressions. The majority visiting Africa's national parks do so expressly hoping to see a kill. Why?

Perhaps, as hunters ourselves, there is some deep empathy with others in the same business. More likely, though, the violence of predation touches those same chords that led people to watch hangings and the Roman games; why watching a murder on television is regarded as entertainment. Perhaps, seeing killers in action, we sublimate hostilities that we feel towards our fellows. No reason is wholly convincing, but lack of explanation does not deny the fact.

In all the wild, nothing attracts us so strongly as the animal hunters going about their work. And in all the world, there is no better place to watch them than in the Serengeti-Mara. The concourse of herbivores there supports many carnivores, from a variety of mongooses, genets and small cats; hyaena, the dogs (wild dog and jackal), to the big felines — lion, leopard and cheetah, atop the pyramids of life. Abundant because of the huge food supply, they are also approachable. So many people come to see them that they have become accustomed to their presence in vehicles. And, because there is so much open country, they are easily visible.

Generally, the bigger vertebrate predators tend to be opportunists and rather unselective in their choice of prey. Inevitably this creates a situation in which hunting species often compete against one another. It would thus be understandable if evolution had resulted in pyramids of life that were dominated by a single carnivore species in any one area. The Serengeti-Mara stands out from this expectation for, rather than having one top predator, it seems to have a parliament of large meat-eaters. Some, like the termite and insect-eating aardwolf, have

Previous pages: The annual wildebeest
migration, considered the world's premier
wildlife spectacle.

become so specialized that they do not compete with others. But lion, leopard, cheetah, wild dog, the three species of jackal (side-striped, black-backed and golden) and the spotted hyaena have widely overlapping interests. Each species, however, has behavioural characteristics that sets it apart from the others.

Lion, by virtue of size, can take animals as large as adult buffalo and giraffe. On occasion they have been known to kill black rhino, and in some areas, such as the Virunga National park in Zaire, they actually specialize in hippo. Leopard, being smaller and far more arboreal, subsist off animals too small to satisfy lion. Yet a leopard has been recorded killing a full-grown bull eland, the largest of the antelope. In very open country, cheetah, with their unique burst of speed, have an advantage over the other two big cats. The unique digestive system of the hyaena allows it to eat bone and waste that would not support other predators. Such specializations are obvious. Each animal may have different preferences in what and how it hunts. Yet overall, the list of their prey contains more common than separate features.

Nothing displays the selectiveness and ecological moulding of the Serengeti-Mara's large carnivores more than their overall distributions and range of habitats. Most widespread and adaptable of all is the leopard. They once occupied all of Africa, much of the Middle East, Pakistan, India, Sri Lanka and the whole of the Indo-Chinese and Malayan region. Today they are absent from North Africa and mostly gone from the Middle East. But elsewhere they still occur widely. And within this huge range they are at home in almost any habitat except true desert and montane snow fields where, even so, the kindred snow leopard has made its home.

Lion and cheetah had similar general distributions. They occupied Africa both north and south of the Sahara, much of the Middle East, Iran and the Indian sub-continent. Lion were once found in Europe, too. Today both are gone from North Africa and the Middle East. A few lion hold out in India's Gir National Park and a small number of cheetah may survive in Iran and southern Russia.

South of the Sahara, however, both species are widespread, only absent on developed farmlands and where there are many people. Their choice of habitat is wide. Lion occur in all but tall forest, true desert and snow fields. In Zambia's Lake Bangweulu they even spend long periods in swamp, stalking lechwe and sitatunga antelope through knee-deep water. Cheetah are more discriminating, avoiding not only tall forests, but all dense vegetation and mountain moorland. Nevertheless, they still exist in a broad range of vegetation and terrain, probably more tolerant of arid areas than either lion or leopard.

Unlike the big cats, spotted hyaena never existed outside Africa. Extinct now in the lower

Following pages: Continued poaching in the Serengeti has sent elephant across the border seeking refuge in the Maasai Mara. Some are aggressive and will charge vehicles or people.

Above: Although poaching in the Maasai Mara is mostly under control, the story across the border is quite different. There is not a single rhino left in the whole of the Serengeti.

Nile valley — the ancient Egyptians considered force-fed hyaena a culinary delicacy — they are still widespread throughout the rest of Africa. Their choice of habitat is as wide as lion, excluding only rain forest and snowfield.

Wild dog have a similar range. Curious to a fault, they will inspect even those environments that hold no promise for them. One was once photographed in the snow on the highest point of Mount Kilimanjaro.

The three species of jackal found in the Serengeti-Mara have a combined distribution in both Africa and Asia nearly as extensive as the leopard. Individually, though, they are not as widespread as the bigger carnivora. The side-striped jackal is the most widespread of the species in Africa. Found south of the Sahara in all but the southernmost part of the continent, it turns up almost everywhere outside the tall rain forests. The black-backed species, more an arid land animal, is found in the Horn of Africa and Eastern Africa; and in the Kalahari, extending into Botswana, Zimbabwe and South Africa. The golden jackal is an Asian and North African species. The Serengeti lies at the southernmost extremity of its range in Africa.

Whatever the ranges and habitat, the big predators adapt their feeding habitats to local circumstances. The lion's choice of young elephant in Malawi is an example of this adaptation. In the Rufiji river basin of Tanzania, the preference is crocodile.

In Addis Ababa, spotted hyaena live off the city's waste. Elsewhere they scavenge other hunters' leftovers. But, as in the Serengeti-Mara, they are also killers in their own right, with no creature — except elephant, perhaps — safe from their attentions. Lion, leopard, jackal and hyaena all come to carrion readily: that way they avoid the dangers and exertions of hunting. But neither cheetah nor wild dog commonly partake of carrion.

All predators take an intense interest in any hunting activity. Lion avidly watch hyaena chasing a wildebeest and vice-versa. When one party makes a kill, others weigh up their chances of driving it off and taking the prey. Thus, when studied more than a decade ago, the lion in Ngorongoro Crater obtained more meat through stealing hyaena kills than they actually caught for themselves. Yet it is not unusual for hyaena to gang up and 'chivvy' lion off what they have caught.

Jackal gather whenever they see one of the larger species hunting. Indeed, watching them you may wonder how the dog first became domesticated. The way they keep an eye on lion and scavenge from under their noses is reminiscent of how domestic dogs follow a hunting party.

Dogs are widely thought to have derived from a Eurasian jackal, and if man became a professional hunter to survive the northern winters, as seems likely, it is easy to imagine the dog's ancestor waiting on the human killers, just as they now attend lion and other hunters in the Serengeti and Mara.

Cheetah and wild dog are exceptions to this rule of theft. While other predator species may try to take over their kills, they seldom do. Cheetah have never been seen to pirate another's quarry and wild dog only once — while Karl and Kathrine Ammann were taking pictures for this book.

The outcome of such opportunism among the Serengeti-Mara's bigger predators is that they compete against one another. Not in simple piracy alone. They also prey on one another. Just as they do with impala, leopard hang cheetah carcasses in trees. Cheetah chase, catch and eat jackal. Lion kill and eat leopard and cheetah. They also kill hyaena and jackal but do not eat them. They are generally hostile towards other predators. Much indicates that cubs of any predator species are at high risk, particularly when still blind. But, though their offspring are vulnerable to others, cheetah and wild dog do not seem to seek out other carnivore cubs.

In view of this, the theory that each predator has a particular niche is unconvincing. It makes for tidy ecology, but nothing else. The point is most clearly made when these carnivores turn their attention to people and domestic stock. Man-eating is still common in East Africa with lion and spotted hyaena the most frequent culprits, followed much less frequently by leopard and a single instance of a wild dog taking a girl. All, including cheetah and jackal, kill livestock. And man is thereby caught in the web of competitive hostility between predators.

The common characteristics — and differences — of the big predators show up in their hunting techniques. Using stealth, like a household cat, the three big cats take advantage of all cover, crouching, freezing, then moving forward as soon as the quarry's attention is elsewhere. Finally, when they can get no closer by stalking, there is an incredibly fast rush and the pounce.

Killing techniques depend upon size. Small animals are bitten through the upper neck or skull. Larger species are thrown to the ground and, by preference, seized by the throat and throttled. Lion and leopard, however, are more varied in technique than cheetah. Being muscular and strong, equipped with big, hooked claws, both are capable of holding and subduing a big animal through brute force. And though they aim to grasp a victim's throat, they may take it by the muzzle and suffocate it, or break its neck by biting or twisting — or, as happens now and then, by simply mauling it to death. Leopard have the added advantage of pouncing on prey from trees.

Cheetah neither have the physical strength nor the hooked claws to hold, overcome and kill a large animal. Their claws retract partially, but are more dog-like in shape than those of a cat. Only the dewclaws on the inside of the 'wrists' are still hooked in the classic cat style. Evolved for high speed sprints, muscles and weight have been sacrificed for lightness. Presumably the need to develop away from more general feline physiology came about through living on flat open land with little cover. The normal stealthy stalk so difficult, the cheetah developed the short rush-and-pounce into a longer sprint. High speed had to be maintained for a distance of several hundred metres rather than ten or twenty paces. The subsequent lack of strength was compensated by refinement in killing technique. This grew out of the pace of the chase. At maximum speed over several hundred metres, it left the victim breathless and exhausted.

When a cheetah closes with its victim, both are still at full speed. It swipes at the prey's rump. As the hooked dewclaw pulls it off balance, the animal tumbles. In a trice the cheetah has it by the throat, keeping its own body well clear of flailing hooves. Windpipe closed, desperate for oxygen, the quarry has no reserves for struggle and is soon unconscious. So essential is the sprint that if an intended victim stands its ground when a cheetah breaks cover, the cat will often call off the hunt.

This specialization, however, puts the cheetah at a singular disadvantage in the situations that prevail in the Serengeti-Mara. Indeed, the species seems to have a marked inferiority complex. With little more than a determined approach, almost any animal, regardless of size, can get cheetah to abandon their kills.

Hyaena, wild dog and jackal use much different procedures. Not for them the long, cautious stalk. Instead, they relentlessly chase their victims over long distances, harrying them to a standstill. But most jackal kills are small species scurrying among the grass stalks — caught with a swift pounce and killed with a nip.

Africa's wild dog are the supreme harriers. The pack singles a victim out of the herd and strings out behind and on either side of it. One or two keep close to the quarry, maintaining a fast run. When they tire, they fall back to be replaced by others who keep up the chase. If the victim tries to break, the dogs on the flanks head it off. Eventually, the pack moves up and the dogs start tearing at the running animal's flanks and hindquarters. Abdomen ripped open, the animal collapses.

As with cheetahs, these relatively small creatures — average weight twenty-five kilos — use the chase to wear down far stronger animals. Attacking flanks and hindquarters, they stay clear of dangerous, horned or toothed 'sharp ends', and of being trodden underneath. In support of one another, the effect is that of a far bigger predator. And, unlike the cheetah, their quarry is not easily taken from them by other meat-eaters.

Following pages: When the rains finally fall, they often transform the plains into a shallow lake.

Superficially somewhat dog-like, spotted hyaena in fact share a distant ancestry with the mongooses, genets and civets. They hunt like dogs, both singly and in packs, and will chase victims over several kilometres of hard running. They kill — usually as fast as lion and leopard strangling their prey — by slashing at the flanks, abdomen and hindquarters.

Social behaviour also reveals the affinities and differences of the large predators. In the basic cat mould, lion, leopard and cheetah are all territorial to a degree. They mark their home ranges with urine, backing up to marker posts and objects in much the same way as a domestic tom. Lion and leopard reinforce this scent trace with sound. Both 'roar', classified by some zoologists in the genus *Panthera*, of which a characteristic is a special arrangement of the throat's hyoid bones enabling them to roar.

The majestic lion's roar is a combination of four or five deep roars spaced by the time that its takes to draw a huge breath, followed by a series of a dozen or more grunts. These progressively decrease in volume and accelerate in tempo. So powerful is this roar that a lion's breath will stir the dust two metres ahead of it. Roaring advertises occupation of territory. Both male and female roar, the sound carrying eight kilometres and more, enabling individual beasts to locate and keep clear of one another.

The leopard's roar, not so loud as the lion, is a succession of deep grunts often likened to a saw cutting through a hollow log. Impressive and sinister, it also serves to proclaim territorial ownership.

All three big cats oust strangers of the same sex from their territories — males objecting to other males, females to other females. If scent and sound warnings are ignored the confrontations become physical. In all three species killing has been witnessed.

Leopard are solitary creatures. Males and females consort only to mate, and families stay together only until the young become independent. Cheetah females are also solitary, meeting males only to mate, and keeping company only while they have immature dependants. Male cheetah may be solitary, but often mix in twos or threes. Lion are the odd cats out in that they like company.

The basic size of a pride is determined by available food. In dry lands where prey is scarce, some prides consist only of a female and her immature young, who leave her as soon as they are old enough. But in other places, such as the Serengeti-Mara, there may be more than fifty in a pride, many of them small cubs. The core of any pride is the females, all likely to be closely related — mothers, daughters, granddaughters, sisters and cousins.

When food is plentiful there is little incentive to leave the family pride or its territory. But males leave their maternal group as they mature to become wanderers. Fully mature lion try

*Above: After giving birth, a Grant's gazelle licks
her offspring to life.*

to take over a pride by ousting its adult males. Those that succeed rule for several years until in turn they are ousted by younger creatures — to end their days as loners or in small bachelor groups of two and three.

Watching jackal you will notice immediately that they behave much the same as their close relatives, domestic dogs. Gregarious and territorial, the basic social unit is a male-female partnership with dependent young. Several pairs may come to feed off kills but, for the most part, each stays within its own boundaries.

African wild dog are also highly gregarious, sometimes found in packs of sixty and more. Such groups were common earlier in the century, but have become progressively rarer, even in the protected environs of the Serengeti-Mara. There could be two reasons for this decline. Wild dog are unpopular with farmers and stockmen and shot on sight. So impressive is their efficiency even earlier conservationists were against them, fearing that they would extermin-ate antelope in national parks — not thinking to consider how the dogs and other animals had interacted through the ages without such a catastrophe. In Uganda, for example, wardens were ordered to kill all wild dog on sight and the species is now extinct in the two major parks, Murchison Falls and Queen Elizabeth, and all but gone from a third park — Kidepo.

Wild dog are also susceptible to canine distemper and rabies. In the past, distemper may

*Following pages: Here, in the short grass plains
of the Serengeti, clutches of teenage ostrich
often form flocks of up to 100 birds.*

have been a rare disease in the wild. Now, with more people and domestic dogs, the infections may have risen to levels that threaten the wild species.

Perhaps the most outstanding aspect of the wild dog communities is the co-operation between pack members. Pups are rapidly weaned and converted to a diet of raw meat. All members bring this food back to the den. By whimpering, begging and poking their muzzles at the corner of the adults' mouths, the pups induce them to regurgigate the meat — so reliable a system that one males-only pack reared a litter after the mother died.

The other beneficiaries of this mutual concern are those who, unable to keep up with the pack, are also fed on the same basis. Perhaps unique among land predators, wild dog often keep injured or sick companions alive until they recover from a hurt that, for any other hunter, would spell the end.

Allied to this close social interdependence is another unusual feature — males often outnumber females to an extraordinary degree. Some packs may contain a dozen males and only one female, but it does not seem to result in competition for her favours. This pronounced differential of sex ratios has not yet been explained.

As social as wild dog, but with very pronounced codes and rules, spotted hyaena are clearly different to dogs or cats in their behaviour. Theirs is a matriarchal, but nonetheless highly territorial society. Bigger than males, females dominate society. Spotted hyaena form clans, each of which has a well-defined territory vigorously defended against members of other clans.

Within its territory a clan will have several dens; usually sets of inter-connecting burrows. Young are born deep underground. Unlike wild dog, however, the pups are not cared for by the whole community. Indeed, in their first weeks mothers strongly discourage interest and close approach by other hyaena, particularly males. Though the manner in which the young are reared differs from that practised by wild dog, it is no less efficient.

Generally, carnivores wean their young early, an advantage exemplified by wild dog. The sooner they eat meat, the sooner the whole pack can shift the load from a single individual, the mother. Hyaena cubs, on the other hand, are not weaned until very late. The implication is that hyaena social organization is so reliable that the young can safely remain dependent on a single individual much longer than any other carnivore species.

Comparing these different species shows how evolution takes different routes to success. In a broader sense, the same point is made by any study of the Serengeti-Mara community. If one species does not exploit an opportunity, others will. In microcosm, they highlight the relentless competition that is such a strong feature of the evolutionary process. Here, as in no other 'laboratory', evolution can be seen in progress, proclaiming constant change. Through observing these processes, the vast record of past life, the countless extinctions recorded by fossils and palaeontology, become understandable.

Some arose when the physical environment changed so drastically that species failed to adapt. Others happened because one species was caught 'looking the wrong way' when an opportunity arose. Before it could collect itself, others moved in.

The idea of balanced nature, of long-term stability, of static systems, grew from observations in the modified habitats of Europe. There were fewer species anyway and those that existed were diminished even more as man shaped the land to suit his purpose. But the delusion grew that nature was constant. The Serengeti-Mara shows otherwise. And, in so doing, gives mankind unique insights into natural life.

Following pages: Hippo clash over territorial
dominance in the Mara River.

The
HUNTERS
and the
HUNTED

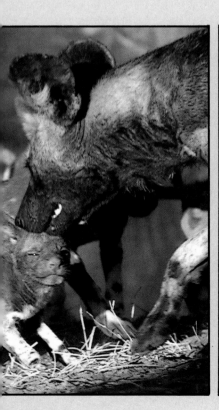

Leopard

Though strikingly obvious at close quarters, the leopard's spotted coats make them difficult to see in the dappling of sunlight. Their pattern is excellent camouflage among leaves. Most solitary, nocturnal and arboreal of Africa's big cats, it's hardly surprising that they are also the least seen. Yet, for those who can read the signs — the spoor along tracks and at watering places — they are also the most widespread and common.

Superb in their cryptic purpose, in modern times leopard skins have brought calamity upon the species. Beautiful, soft and silky, they were much sought after as a fashion fur. Demand exceeded supply. In the Serengeti-Mara leopard numbers dropped. Public opinion, however, turned against the vogue for leopard skin coats and handbags and effectively killed the trade. Since the mid-1970s leopard numbers in some of the affected areas have recovered to the point where, as in the Serengeti-Mara, they are now common.

Distributed throughout Africa and Asia, leopard have the largest range of all the world's great cats. But there are marked regional differences in size and colouring. Throughout savannah Africa, the standard pattern of a yellow background, with smallish, black rosettes, prevails. In the forests of Asia the background colour may be deep russet with far larger black markings. In both Asia and highland Ethiopia, entirely black specimens are common.

Above: Female leopard finishes off an impala meal in a tree on Rhino Ridge, Maasai Mara.

Opposite: Female and cub, 'treed' by a pride of lion, watching the lion retreat.

Previous pages: Leopard in a tree demonstrates nature's artistry at camouflage.

Right: Young male leopard scent-marks a tree. But the resident patriarch, probably its father, will soon tell him in no uncertain terms to move on.

By their movements and attitude leopard appear bigger than they actually are. But slightness of physical size is not reflected by lack of courage or ferocity. Before firearms were introduced to Kenya, young Maasai and Kalenjin warriors sometimes destroyed stock-killing lion and leopard by surrounding them, closing in and spearing the culprits. Invariably, the victims charged the ring of men. The man at the point of the charge tried to take it on his shield, keeping it between himself and the angry cat. And as the cat concentrated fully on one man, his companions speared it. The system worked moderately well with lion, for they would worry at the man behind the shield. As often as not, he was severely mauled, but it left the animal vulnerable to the other spearmen. With leopard it was a swat here,

a bite there — the smaller, more agile carnivore didn't concentrate on one victim and ran up a longer list of casualties.

Surprisingly their weight is similar to a full-grown person — males average sixty kilos (132 lbs.) with a range of between thirty-seven and ninety kilos (eighty-one lbs. and 200 lbs.). Slightly smaller, females average fifty kilos (110 lbs.), ranging between twenty-eight and sixty kilos (sixty-two and 132 lbs.). Generally, leopard in forests and wetter areas are bigger than those in arid regions. Leopard in the Serengeti-Mara tend to be in the middle of the size range.

Basically loners, leopard behave rather like domestic cats. Both males and females establish territories that they seldom leave, which vary in size from under ten to over

fifty square kilometres. The availability of food and prey may have some bearing on the size of territory. Where food is abundant they are likely to be small; and large where it is scarce. Territories tend to overlap. In particular, a male beat may overlap those of several females. Nevertheless, individuals tend to avoid one another. Each notifies its presence by scent-marking in typical cat manner. They also advertise themselves through their loud and distinctive call.

Other leopard hearing this call mostly take note and steer clear. Like tom-cats, however, males do not always avoid one another. From the scars that are common about their heads and necks, it seems they often fight.

During the last two decades, trouble-

some leopard — for example, those that kill livestock — have been caught and translocated to national parks, rather than destroyed. But recent research now indicates that this has been a largely pointless exercise. Scientist Patrick Hamilton fitted radio collars to several leopard released in Kenya's Meru National Park. None stayed. They all made long journeys out of the park. With a cat's homing instinct, they headed back to where they had come from. Their reactions make territorial sense. The released leopard probably felt uncomfortable in the midst of many strange leopard territories. At the very least, their rapid movement can be interpreted as seeking an unoccupied place in which to settle.

Above: A female leopard spots potential prey and starts the stalk.

Above: Leopard stalk by slinking through the high grass, using cover effectively. In the Mara they rarely use trees from which to launch themselves on unsuspecting victims.

The first leopards are thought to have been forest dwellers. Since then the species has adapted to an exceptionally wide range of habitats. The only big feline to occupy Africa's true forests, it is also at home in thickets and grasslands, alpine moorland and sea-shores, and in the wettest and virtually driest areas. No other carnivore of its size is quite so widespread. One key to this striking adaptability is the variety of food leopard eat. At the bottom of the menu, by no means the rarest item, is carrion. These cats are inveterate scavengers. They readily eat other meat than their own kills, no matter how rotten it might be. Of course, this is their Achilles' heel, for it means that they can be baited and easily poisoned. If sportsmen had to stalk leopard, they would be among the most difficult trophies to obtain. But because they can be drawn to a cache of smelly meat, all the hunter has to do is lie in wait, well concealed, and the trophy will come to

him. As a result, leopard are relatively easy prey for both sportsman and poacher.

At the other end of their diet, leopard catch and kill animals much bigger than themselves. One victim, a full-grown bull eland, was perhaps ten times a leopard's weight. Instances in which such a large quarry is taken are extremely rare. Man-eating is common in certain parts of Africa — southern Tanzania and western Kenya, for example — and in India, people are killed and eaten regularly. During an eight-year spell — between 1918 and 1926 — the most famous of these Indian leopard, the Man-eater of Rudraprayag, took more than 125 people, avoiding the concerted efforts of both the local community and the Government to destroy it.

Leopard also take small species — rats and mice, for instance — but such feeding is seldom seen. The victim, caught with a pounce, is swallowed at a gulp.

Patrick Hamilton found that eighteen per

cent of leopard dung in Tsavo, Kenya, contained arthropod remains: grasshoppers, centipedes and scorpions. And in thirty-five per cent there were rodent remains. Leopard are also known to eat flying termites, beetles, spiders, snakes, lizards, fish, birds, shrews, gerbils, hare, spring hare, hyrax, wart hog, bush pig, baboon, monkey, chimpanzee, gorilla, dik-dik, duiker, klipspringer, Thomson's and Grant's gazelle, impala, reedbuck, bushbuck, lesser kudu, waterbuck, eland, giraffe, jackal, lion cubs, cheetah, sheep, goats, cattle, domestic dogs and domestic cats; and at least one case of cannibalism is known. Hyaena have been killed by leopard, but left uneaten. In a nutshell, a hungry leopard will take virtually whatever is on offer. But individuals do develop preferred tastes. Jonathan Kingdon, the artist and zoologist, knew of one in Uganda which ignored abundant goats in favour of domestic dogs.

Together with its secretiveness and excellent camouflage, this universal range of food must play an important role in the leopard's widespread success. Long after other large mammals — herbivores as well as carnivores — have abandoned an area because of human settlement, leopard remain. Scavenging, catching rats, mice, dogs and feral cats, they live amid dense populations. In Nairobi, in the 1960s, a captive leopard escaped into the town. Many traps were set but it eluded recapture. To the astonishment of all, however, two totally wild leopard were caught.

In May 1986, an adult female was caught in a wire snare set for a small antelope in Nairobi's Langata suburb. Two years earlier a full-grown leopard was killed in the centre of Harare, Zimbabwe.

Given this ability, it's very surprising man-eating is not more common.

Above: Once a predator is spotted, the stalk is abandoned and the intended prey often moves in for a closer look at the intruder.

The actual killing technique of the leopard depends to some degree upon the victim's size: small animals are bitten through the upper neck or head, larger victims may have their necks wrenched and broken by the forepaws. Far more commonly, however, they are bitten through the throat. The long dagger-like canines sever major blood vessels to the brain and the grip quickly chokes the prey. This hold calls for little exertion once the quarry is down and is widely used by all the big cats. The photographs on this and the facing page show a leopard, a lioness and a cheetah using the throat hold.

Leopard are stealthy hunters. When they stalk they seem almost to flow around and over obstacles. Finally, within a few paces of their prey, there is a lightning rush and the victim is seized by powerfully hooked forepaws, held in a lethal embrace and bitten. The momentum usually slams all but the largest animals to the ground. Those that resist the initial impact are dragged down.

Below: Lioness uses throat hold to suffocate a wildebeest.

Bottom: Cheetah suffocating a female impala.

Opposite: Leopard kill small prey by biting them through the neck. Large victims are suffocated with a throat hold.

Below: Female leopard carries a duiker kill back to her cubs.

Though they are supreme predators, leopard themselves also fall victim to others. Young cubs are most vulnerable. To feed, mothers must periodically leave their small cubs alone. Artful concealment helps reduce discovery, but even so they may fall to a range of passing carnivores that vary from the bigger eagles to jackal and lion. In the Serengeti-Mara the large hyaena population poses the greatest threat to young cubs.

All leopard are under permanent threat from lion. The two species show a marked intolerance to one another. Because of the difference in size, leopard usually keep clear of lion. Their normal reaction on seeing a lion is to seek refuge in a tree or dense cover. On two occasions we recorded apparently sleepy lion lying at the base of a tree in which a leopard was hiding. Both times the leopard fled when a vehicle approached and each time it was chased by the lion. In one case the leopard escaped. In the other it was torn to pieces. An implacable hatred seems to exist between the two. While all leopard have a natural tendency to stay close to cover, the large numbers of lion in the Serengeti-Mara give this instinct added impetus.

Another risk that leopard share with all predators that hunt large quarry is the danger of being hurt when trying to subdue a big, powerful victim. And though injured lion, hyaena, jackal, wild dog, and even male cheetah can get through by sharing kills, for all are communal to a degree, the lonely leopard does not have this option. The individual that cannot kill is doomed. In the highly competitive Serengeti-Mara, wounded creatures are watched carefully — particularly by the hyaena. When sufficiently weakened they end up as prey.

Above: Leopard cub awaits arrival of mother in the early morning light.

Above: Female leopard of about six — in her prime and a successful mother.

Watching leopard cubs in constant and close contact with their mother and one another it is difficult to think of them as solitary. Rubbing against each other in sensual abandon, just as domestic cats do to their owners, implies pleasure in company and a strong incentive to stay sociable.

When ready to mate, female leopard advertise the fact by frequent scent markings rapidly picked up by any males whose territories overlap. The normal solitude lapses and both male and female actively seek the companionship of the opposite sex. Under female allure, males often go beyond their normal borders and fight rivals. Once they have made contact they remain for what may well be two weeks of courtship and mating. The she-leopard may go with the male to those parts of his range that do not touch hers. During this time the two often share kills and hunt together.

When she is off heat they go their respective ways. If the female conceives, gestation takes about 100 days. Cubs are born in litters of between two and six in the deepest cover — caves, rocky crevices, aardvark burrows, hollow logs and the like. Blind

and helpless like domestic kittens, the cubs are surprisingly small. They grow fast and their eyes open during their second week. By their second month they start to eat meat and are completely weaned in their third month though still weighing less than three kilos (6.6 lbs.).

But the young, vulnerable to a host of other predators, are still kept under cover near the natal lair. During this time the mother brings kills to them, or as close as she can.

By four months the cubs are agile enough to climb and feed off kills stashed in trees. Even so, they have to be hidden while she hunts. Already, evidence of their solitary instinct has begun to show, particularly when feeding. There is little gentility or sharing. Each competes for the food with much growling and spitting. The larger males are most successful and by six months one member of the litter may be twice as large as its siblings.

We watched a family's disintegration at Rhino Ridge. The first signs came from the cubs when they were a year old. Each appeared to be 'doing its own thing' just that little bit more, and progressively seemed less compelled to stay close to the

others. The young male started calling in true leopard fashion for the first time. For all the world like a youth overcome with pride in his breaking voice, he called frequently as though he couldn't hear enough of himself.

The cubs' growing independence was most marked during rest periods. Instead of lying up together, they went their independent ways, often ending up several hundred metres apart. Curiously, despite the distance between them, their mother seemed to know where each was. When the time came to make a move she would set off towards one, then another and finally the last, calling and gathering them to her, even though she couldn't see where they had been lying up. As always, their greetings were full of affection and much physical contact. Though they were starting to drift apart, there seemed no decline in their pleasure at the closeness of other members. There was no evidence that the youngsters were being forced away from their mother. The process appeared gentle, with little loss of 'friendship'.

Newly on their own, once more the young are vulnerable. Inept at hunting, without an established territory, they fall on hard times. We once followed such a 'teenager' hunting in daylight. It signalled his hunger. He investigated every bush, clump of grass or cover that he came upon over several miles of open country, hoping to find something to catch and eat. Twice he flushed hares but, even though one only went a short distance before freezing, he was too inept to catch it. Finally, he stuck his head into a burrow that contained a wart hog. It should have been a certain catch. But when the hog shot out of its hole the young leopard leapt aside. It is during this period of early independence that these drifting youngsters are most likely to be killed by their implacable enemy — the lion.

By the time they are a year old, most cubs have started catching prey — albeit small animals such as rats and lizards. The process of independence has begun. It may take months, with mother and young spending less and less time in one another's company until they only meet to share a kill. Complete independence probably starts when the female once more comes into heat, seeks a mate and starts all over again.

Above: Curious leopard cub returns the stares of watching tourists.

When water is available, leopard drink regularly and often. Damp earth about pool edges and along river banks are good places to look for their footprints. But they also live months at a time without drinking. This indicates that they can obtain enough liquid for their needs from their kills.

Yet much remains to be learned. Leopard are the least researched of Africa's big cats. In Eastern Africa, the only extended investigation into leopard biology was made by Patrick Hamilton in Kenya's Tsavo National park in the 1970s.

He placed radio collars on a number of individuals, enabling him to follow their movements over a number of months. Even with a constant radio signal indicating the precise location of a marked animal, it was often difficult to actually see the leopard. Little wonder that the species has been neglected. Most zoologists want to study subjects that will yield results with some certainty and in some quantity.

There are records of leopard tame enough to allow people in motor vehicles to approach closely. Invariably these have occurred where there are many visitors and an attractive habitat — the trees along the water courses about Seronera, headquarters of the Serengeti National Park, form such a place and created some very tame leopard. But this gave the false impression that there were many leopard. In fact, the animals involved were few, and far more leopard will have seen people than were seen.

The Mara, with its tourists, open grasslands, and abundant prey, is a good place to watch leopard; probably the best in Africa. With so many people and so few places to hide, the spotted cats have become tame. Although this may be good for the tourists, it also exposes leopard to their competitors — lion, hyaena, jackal and others — which in the long run may not be quite such a good thing.

Above: Carcass of a Thomson's gazelle hangs in a tree, an effective storage system.

When a leopard cannot eat its kill quickly or at one sitting it tries to get the carcass under cover. Not only is it more comfortable to eat in shade, but it reduces the chances of unwelcome guests arriving to share the meal. After eating, what remains must be cached for further meals, for there would be small point in a solitary animal killing prey as big or bigger than itself if most of the carcass only benefitted others. The leopard's climbing ability enables it to hide carcasses up trees where few other meat-eaters can get at them. Their great strength is put to its fullest test in wedging dead animals in forks far from the ground. It calls for an agility that has its roots far back in cubhood. A great deal of juvenile play involves climbing — and the mother often participates.

Leopard, lion, hyaena, jackal, vultures, tawny and bateleur eagles are incorrigible pirates, ever on the lookout for free meals. Well-versed in one another's ways, they automatically watch their fellow meat-eaters. The low-flying bateleur can see much of what goes on under cover and is continually watched by higher-flying vultures. Any break in its long cross-country traverses, any circling to get a better look at something beneath it, catches their attention. And when it descends, down come the vultures for a closer look. When they lose height rapidly, the earth-bound buccaneers watch them. Only cheetah and wild dog are indifferent to what the others are doing or what they may have killed.

In three instances, the female leopard at Rhino Ridge, which on two occasions drove a cheetah off its kill, lost her own kills to the resident hyaena clan. Indeed, such was their vigilance that unless she could get her kills up in a tree they benefitted far more than she from her hunting. This implies that in the Serengeti-Mara, where hyaena are extremely common, they must deter any leopard from living far from rocks and trees.

Watching, but unseen, unmoving for hours on end, leopard rest through the day's hot hours. An ideal spot will overlook the surrounding land in the shade of overhanging rocks, high up on a hillside, or, where the land is flat, in the canopy of a tall tree. They are most often seen in the early mornings or late evenings, when the sun is gentle, relaxing in a favourite tree.

Animals accustomed to frequent human contact not only become tame, but sometimes turn the association to their advantage. Leopard, lion and cheetah have all been recorded using slow-moving vehicles as stalking-horses to get close to prey. Antelope and others that associate cars with noisy visitors but no other trouble are easy victims for a predator that suddenly rushes from behind a rank of vehicles.

But normally predators besieged by tourists lie still and sleep out the ordeal, giving the impression that the animals either don't mind the presence of people or can't recognize a person inside a vehicle. Leopard have given the lie to this. In the Mara, some are so used to vehicles that they lie in full view. But on two occasions in 1986, 'tame' leopards lost their temper. They jumped into open-top vehicles and attacked the noisy occupants. Luckily, no one was killed, but the victims were severely mauled.

Below: While vultures do not profit from leopard kills stored in trees, a tawny eagle finds an easy meal on a favourite perch.

Opposite: Sitting on a gazelle kill, a leopard takes a nap.

Right: Although about eighteen months old and nearly mature, these three leopard cubs still seem comfortable in each other's company.

Above: Leopard mother and cub enjoy a play session.

Opposite: Playful cub swats aloof mother with a gentle paw.

Above: Young martial eagle takes off.

Apart from the bateleur, the martial eagle is probably the most aerial of all Africa's eagles. It spends most of the day soaring so high it is invisible to all but the keenest human eye. So normally the bird is seen when it is not flying — conspiciously perched on a dead tree or a bare branch.

The martial eagle is relatively common in the Serengeti-Mara. As with many birds of prey, the female is bigger than the male by as much as a third: it may weigh six kilos (thirteen lbs.) with a wingspan of up to 2.6 metres (8.5 feet).

Like the leading carnivores in the ecosystem, martial eagles are remarkably universal in their choice of prey, although apparently they do not scavenge. Their favourite quarry seems to be game birds about the size of guinea fowl, but they have

been seen taking francolins, bustards, white storks, Egyptian geese, poultry, young ostriches, ground squirrels, mongooses, genets, hare, hyrax, jackal cubs, full-grown caracal (African lynx), lambs, kids, young antelope up to the size of half-grown impala and monitor lizards. And, given the chance, martial eagles will kill small cubs — lion, leopard, cheetah and hyaena.

Kills small enough to be carried are taken to a nearby perch or, when breeding, to the nest. If too heavy to lift, they are eaten on the spot. Like leopard, martial eagles return to a big kill over several days. In the Serengeti-Mara, however, it is unlikely that other scavengers give them the opportunity to do this.

They hunt in two ways. The more usual

is a long, shallow dive over a considerable distance, wings partly furled and rigid; no wing beats catch the victim's eye — just a silhouette swiftly growing larger. By the time its speed and direction are apparent it is too late. As the broad wings and tail flare in a dramatic braking movement, the great taloned feet reach forwards — seizing the victim in an immensely strong grasp and driving the inch-long claws deep into the body. Death is almost instantaneous.

The other method for them is to sit quietly in a tree, then drop swiftly onto any unwary animal that comes within reach below.

Like many eagles, martials mate for long periods, if not for life. The same nest site is used year after year and the nests develop into substantial structures — up to two metres (6.6 feet) in diameter and more than one metre (3.3 feet) deep. They are usually set high above ground, in the fork of a tree, more often than not located on a steep hill.

One egg is laid at a time — pale green or bluish-white, splotched with brown and grey. The female, which does most of the incubation, is fed throughout the fifty-day period by her mate. The young eagle leaves its nest about one hundred days after hatching, but continues to be fed by its parents for at least three months. The plumage of the young is light brown above and snowy-white below. The adult is a darker brown, and the white underparts are dotted with brown spots.

Above: Efficient killers, martial eagles surprise their prey in a sudden swoop, using their talons to immobilize and kill.

Lion

Above: Lioness settles down during the heat of the day.

Opposite: Lion spend much of the day lazing and sleeping.

Previous pages: Lioness pauses for a moment's refreshment on her way across a river.

Counterpoint to the secretiveness and solitary nocturnal ways of the leopard is the lion — the most visible, gregarious and noisiest of cats. For sheer volume a lion's roar has few equals. The cat's ferocity and strength are much admired. Perhaps it is this extrovert behaviour that has so impressed itself on mankind. No other animal has been so widely used as an emblem.

Foremost in this symbolism must be the lion's aura of power, self-confidence and strength. The slow swagger of a full-maned lion in its prime, enhanced by the massive-maned head, akin to a patriarch's flowing locks and beard, exudes dignity.

Among the many titles of the Emperors of Ethiopia was the 'Lion of Judah'. The King of the Baganda walked with an odd stiff-legged gait to imitate a lion's stately walk. The badge of the British Empire was a lion and today, as through a thousand years and more of European heraldry, the lion indicates high social status and royalty. Many religious cults have been devoted to lion worship, and the Sphinx, one of the largest statues ever made, is a lion with a human face.

Modern research has knocked some of the glamour and debunked some of the myths, too. Lion, for instance, are carrion eaters by choice — a sad letdown. Yet, despite their now being among the best understood of large wild animals, their mystique survives. You only need to gaze into the terrible intensity of a lion's stare to realize that historical perspectives have a large element of truth.

Above: A purpose for everything — lion's mane provides an important protective cushion in violent fights.

Previous pages: Lion contest supremacy in ferocious combat.

To gain a place in a pride the lion in his prime must displace the incumbent male or males. The big prides so characteristic of the Serengeti-Mara are usually 'owned' by partnerships of up to four males. Uncontested vacancies are few. (Hunters who shoot lion for sport create vacancies.) When it comes to challenging males for a pride, partners fare better than lone individuals. Often, evictions are only achieved through savage and occasionally fatal fighting.

On the southern plains, we see one such fight. It looks as if the lion are nomads fighting over a female. At first, the older male lies close to the female, the other some thirty paces away. The female moves off from our approaching vehicle on a course

that takes her towards the second lion, closely followed by her apparent consort.

Within ten paces, the consort charges the male-in-waiting. Growling prodigiously, they rear up, batting one another with their forepaws before tumbling over, wrestling and biting. The encounter lasts no more than thirty seconds before the younger male canters after the female, which has trotted away during the fracas. After covering several hundred metres, the pair settle down. The new partner licks a leg wound as the former consort gallops up, throwing himself at the younger animal. The fight is even more intense: terrible growling, biting, clawing and kicking. The female makes off again, and the fight breaks up.

This time the older lion runs and rejoins her. Badly bitten, the younger suitor follows the couple with a severe limp — at a respectful distance.

In the Serengeti-Mara, there are two distinct societies of lion — those that are resident year-round, and those that are nomadic, following the migration during its yearly movements. Strongly territorial, invariably part of a settled pride, residents resent strangers. Females will evict strange females, but not males: males evict strange males, but tolerate alien females. Nomads that continually traverse occupied territories do so with considerable discretion. As with many cats, lion mark their home range with scent-marking and much roaring.

The roar enables a pride to keep in contact — and warns non-members to avoid them. Both sexes roar, and members of a pride apparently recognize the call of each individual.

Females in a pride are born into a family group they may never leave. Males, however, leave their maternal prides at about the age of three — sometimes alone, or with brothers and cousins of the same age. Such partnerships often last long. They become nomads, following the game, trespassing quietly on established lion territories. But when they reach full maturity after another two years they set about joining a pride.

Above: Lion fight for domain in savage — and sometimes fatal — battles.

Below: Scent plays a vital role in lion mating. A lion establishes that the lioness is on heat.

Right: Lion copulate with astonishing frequency over long periods of time.

If lion fight ferociously, they mate stupendously. The sensuality and lasciviousness of a lioness on heat is announced by scent and restless demeanour. Waving her tail high, like a domestic cat rubs against the legs of its owner, she rubs herself against her choice among the pride males. Crouching in front of the lion, she solicits endlessly and with such intensity no male can hold out. In thrall, the chosen mate closely follows his feminine suitor. Other pride males usually do not attempt to compete or interfere, though if for some

reason a courting lion is removed, another quickly takes its place.

The season lasts from as little as a single day to the prodigious span of three weeks, during which time they copulate with abandon. Studying lion in the Serengeti, one zoologist recorded that this took place about four times an hour throughout. In Dresden Zoo, Germany, one pair copulated 360 times in eight days — an average of once every half hour. But the performance is accompanied by much rowdy behaviour — the lioness frequently attacks

and swats her suitor between bouts and makes much noise.

In most other animals, except man, copulation is not protracted or drawn-out. Indeed, a single coupling is all that is needed by many species. Of course, it is possible that promiscuous behaviour by the lioness reduces the prospect of violent competition between males, though it doesn't always succeed. The fact that it takes around 1,500 copulations for successful conception suggests that lions have an extremely low level of fertility.

Above: Lioness co-ordinate birth times, and litters of the same age group are allowed to suckle different mothers.

Lioness gestate for 110 days. When ready to give birth, the female seeks a secluded den, deep in a thicket, rock crevice or cave, and retires from normal pride life. Up to nine cubs may be born, though the more usual litter is two to four. Like leopard, the cubs are blind, totally defenceless and weigh two kilos (4.4 lbs.) or less. For their first two months they stay in the natal den before starting to follow their mother and joining the family pride.

Often the females of one pride come into heat at about the same time and give birth in succession. There are advantages. Several females within a pride lactate at the same

time, and if one is unable to produce milk, or dies, her offspring can suckle from any other female in milk. Unlike female leopard that lactate for about three months, lioness remain in milk for up to eight months. This means that even when the cubs start eating meat at around two months, they still supplement their diet with milk.

But this picture of a thoroughly social animal, in which pride families care for one another's cubs, is completely reversed by lion eating etiquette. At a kill the strongest gets the most. In times of scarcity, cubs starve. As with many other youngsters, they are also prone to a variety of hazards,

Above: Snarling lioness chastises playful cub.

the foremost of which is falling prey to another predator. Animals which kill lion cubs include hyaena, leopard, jackal, martial eagles — and the dreadful driver ants which, in their millions, can overcome most mammals that are unable to escape.

Probably unique to lion is a high incidence of cannibalism and infanticide. Established pride males are extremely tolerant of family cubs, but this does not extend to males that have newly taken over a pride. They tend to kill any small cubs in the group. Sometimes the dead cubs are eaten. By the time their own cubs arrive, however, they have become tolerant patriarchs. Biologist Brian Bertram, who studied lion in the Serengeti, interpreted this unattractive behaviour as a form of competition — by getting rid of their rivals' offspring, incoming lion set about fixing their own genetic stamp on the pride.

George Schaller, the doyen of Serengeti lion researchers, estimated that lion cub mortality ran at nearly seventy per cent. Those that survive are full grown at four years, though able to kill for themselves and contribute to the pride's nutrition by the time they are two.

Above: Lioness normally remain members of the pride in which they are born. Many are related and seem to enjoy each other's company.

In 1896, when Britain began to build a railway from Mombasa on the Indian Ocean shores to Lake Victoria, some 1,000 kilometres inland, the engineers encountered many problems — none more bizarre than the Man-eaters of Tsavo.

When the railway entered this area it was a wilderness of *Commiphora* scrub and thicket since opened into grassland by elephants. Even before the railway reached the banks of the Tsavo river, it had a sinister reputation. Many people at this spot had disappeared mysteriously. When the large labour force arrived to build a bridge, the workers also began to disappear.

Two man-eating lion regularly stalked into the labour camps at night to drag victims from their tents — no matter how robust the thorn barricade around the campsite. So demoralized were the railway gangs that they refused to work. Credited with supernatural powers, the two lion were held to be the spirits of former African elders protecting tribal lands from aliens. The bridge that should have taken four months to complete took nearly a year. Eventually the two lion were shot by Colonel J. H. Patterson, the engineer in charge.

In the light of recent insight into lion behaviour, it is easy to see how the environment created the incentive for this slaughter.

Tsavo is a dry area, incapable of sustaining great numbers of prey. As a result, its lion are opportunists that take whatever comes. The major caravan route that crossed their territory must have been a source of much prey — in the form of caravan

porters. The rail gangs greatly increased the numbers. Famine also lay across the land and destitute tribesmen hung about all the railway encampments for hand-outs, scraps and help. Not surprisingly, the lion developed into man-eaters. Indeed, simultaneously there were many instances of man-eating elsewhere along the line — though never to the same extent.

Practice made the Tsavo man-eaters proficient, just as it does those Serengeti-Mara prides that specialize in killing buffalo, or the Malawi lion that take young elephant. These hunters, tackling big and extremely dangerous prey, learn by painful experience when to let go a struggling victim to avoid an avenging elephant's tusks, returning when attention is diverted by another lion.

So they learn to dodge or avoid a dangerous human — the silent wakeful person who lies in wait and fires a shot that wounds or frightens.

Patterson's first attempts to come to grips with the lion bear study. Each near miss the lion experienced was a lesson that only served to educate. Little wonder they became more cunning and proficient as time went on. A famous ex-poacher and game warden, the late J. A. Hunter, claimed that there would never have been such slaughter if Patterson had set a series of simple gun-traps — instead of using the 'sporting' technique such as sitting up at night and trying to shoot the lion or tracking them in the daylight.

Below: A curious youngster sends herd of zebra scurrying.

Below: The chase ends with a reprimand from mother. . .

No young creature is more curious than a lion cub. In the late morning a pride lies asleep under a tree in full view of a herd of zebra. A bored cub looks up and sees the zebra. Curious, it investigates. The zebra see it coming and snort in alarm. They take a few paces, turning to face it. The process is repeated. The cub is alert and excited. It continues the advance, moving further and further away from the safety of the pride. Though it is unlikely he will be kicked by a zebra, now separated from his family and in open ground he is easy prey for another predator. But his mother awakens and brings him back to the shade — and sanctuary.

Below: . . . and the errant cub is escorted back to the pride.

Above: Steely stare of the amber-eyed lion.

An adult lion weighs up to 240 kilos (525 lbs.) and a lioness up to 180 kilos (400 lbs.), both nearly four times as heavy as their leopard counterpart. With such large bodies to fuel, they cannot waste time killing small animals. Where they can, lion tend to specialize in the type of prey they take. It's not only apparent between different areas but between different prides in the same area. In the Mara one specializes in buffalo, another nearby in giraffe. In Zaire's Virunga National Park, lion frequently kill young hippo. In the Rufiji basin in Tanzania they specialize in crocodile. On the fringes of the Kalahari, it's porcupine. These apparent fads, in part, may simply reflect the availability of prey and man-eating should be considered in this context.

But lion remain ever opportunists. They take what comes their way and readily eat carrion. Piracy is common.

Opposite: During the dry season, yellow grass forms a perfect camouflage for lion stalking their prey.

Previous pages: Lion pride rest between digging and with typical feline expectancy wait for the prey to emerge from its den.

Opposite: The hungry pride begins to feast on the still-kicking corpse.

Below: When the wart hog emerges it is swiftly seized . . . and (bottom) despatched.

Lion and lioness, members of a pride of thirteen in poor condition, pursue a wart hog aroused from its siesta. The hog heads for a burrow, arriving well ahead of the pride. A swift 'hand-brake' turn and it shoots backwards down the hole — wart hogs always reverse underground so that their 'sharp' ends face any pursuer. The lion gather round and three adult lioness poke their heads in turn into the burrow — only to withdraw hurriedly. They have come face to face with the wart hog's razor-sharp tushes. As many a predator has found to its cost, a wart hog can rip an assailant open from stem to stern.

Now some young males begin to dig at the roof of the tunnel. At times three work, all in one another's way, at other times all lie around panting in the noontime heat. After ninety minutes part of the tunnel roof caves in. The alarmed hog decides to bolt. It emerges like a champagne cork, but in a trice one lion has it by the throat. Even before it is dead, others grip it by its limbs and any other available hold and tear it asunder.

When a young giraffe is attacked by lion, the commitment to take pictures and not interfere is severely tested. Of all savannah fauna, giraffe are surely the most inoffensive. Surrounded by a pride, this mother and calf are caught away from cover. For as long as the mother stands over the calf, the lion hold their distance. But now she turns her back and takes a few paces, signalling the calf to follow. It tries, but in a flash a lion darts in and claws heavily at the calf's hindquarters. Wheeling, the mother charges back, giving a mooing bellow — a sound rarely heard. With great forward kicks of her forehooves, she drives the lion back and stands again over the wounded calf. When she tries to move off again the process is repeated. This time a lion savages the calf's neck and it bleeds freely. Again the mother rescues it. Nonchalantly, the lion lie around, watching. Again the mother tries to lead an escape, but the weakened youngster can only stagger. This triggers a communal response from the lion. The calf goes down. The mother wheels but doesn't charge. Instead, she canters around the flurry of feeding bodies, two lion at her heels. Now she runs off a little way, pauses and returns to stand silent as the pathetic carcass is ripped apart.

Opposite: Mother guards badly-mauled giraffe.
Top right: But soon the guard slips.
Middle right: Still the mother returns to chase them off the corpse. . .
Bottom right: . . . until the lion begin to feast.

Above: Lioness kills buffalo by holding the muzzle to suffocate it.

Lion hunt alone and together. Tactics are typically cat-like: creeping, belly to the ground, holding still at any sign of suspicion, using whatever cover and concealment is available, then a final rush from within twenty paces or so. Several lion may approach a victim on a wide front and, if it flees, there's always a chance that it will run into one of the others. Where prey is abundant in open country, as in the Serengeti-Mara, these co-operative hunts are more successful than solitary stalks. Occasionally, lion lie in ambush about a waterhole.

On 7 July 1981, along a lugga to the east of Rhino Ridge in the Maasai Mara, we spotted two large male lion trotting parallel to us across the plains. We followed them. Every 100 metres or so they stopped and

listened before continuing. After about a kilometre or so they intersected the lugga and disappeared in bush cover. We drove to the bushes and, although we could see nothing, heard heavy movements. Slowly moving into the cover, between and over some bushes, we found fifteen lion surrounding a group of three bull buffalo. They stood in the centre facing their adversaries. A minute later we saw another large bull, half hidden by bushes, lying on the ground. Although we could see no injuries, the animal was either wounded or sick. Whenever a lion advanced, it triggered a charge by one of the bulls and retreated.

Suddenly one of the buffalo stood facing us, nose in the air. Then he shook his head and moved off through the bushes followed by his two mates. The lion moved in

from all sides on the remaining bull which shook its head a few times as the cats started clawing its rump. Finally a lioness walked up to its head, put both paws around its muzzle and, standing on her hind legs, buried her teeth in it. After about four minutes the old bull collapsed on its side.

Killing techniques vary, but the first move is to seize a victim with the forepaws and throw it to the ground. As it loses balance, the lion or one of its accomplices takes a fatal hold on the throat and strangles it. A common tactic is to hold the victim's muzzle within the mouth and suffocate it. With larger animals — young elephant, buffalo, black rhino and sometimes hippo — lion may simply maul their prey, attacking from different directions,

especially from behind, clawing and biting it until loss of blood and exhaustion brings it down. They may even start feeding before it is dead.

Though buffalo are frequent victims, they sometimes turn the tables. There are many instances of buffalo chasing lion and sometimes killing them. If lion get to a herd from downwind unobserved and seize a victim, the buffalo usually run off in confusion. Should the lion fail to kill quickly, however, and the quarry has time to bellow, the herd may return to its rescue. Once we saw a lame female buffalo, limping behind the herd, grabbed by a pride. But the herd saw what was happening and rushed back *en masse*, scattering the lion in all directions.

Above: A buffalo herd regroups after a lion attack, and returns to chase off the predator. Sometimes they keep lion at bay, watching over a carcass for hours.

The most frequently seen eagle in the Serengeti-Mara is the tawny eagle.

Like predatory mammals, most raptors also defend territories. Once we noticed some birds of prey tumbling in the sky. As we got closer, we saw them drop to the ground.

One sat on the sideline while another one sat on the feet of the third bird. It was screeching and extremely submissive, but its adversary kept hammering away at its feet. Every now and then it would interrupt the attack to glare at the victim.

The end of this interaction came when, out of nowhere, three wild dog appeared on the scene. They chased the birds back into the air and checked the ground for a carcass. They had obviously seen the birds tumble to the ground and decided to find out if there was a kill.

Ornithologists told us it is probable that the eagle under attack was the offspring of the pair and the father had decided that it was time for the son to look for his own territory — and as such expressed its feelings in no uncertain terms.

Opposite: Two tawny eagles, among the most common of the Maasai Mara raptors.

Below: Tawny eagles in territorial dispute.

Below bottom: One adversary keeps hammering away at the invader's feet.

Wild Dog

Above: Wild dog often mark their territories — and relieve an itch — by lying on their backs and pedalling their feet in the air.

Previous pages: Wild dog pack at play.

Of all Africa's predators, none has been more abused or misunderstood than the wild or Cape hunting dogs. Wherever the white man went in Africa, he persecuted them. Even George Adamson of *Born Free* fame admits shooting them out of hand. Conservation organizations actually requested all and sundry to shoot dogs whenever possible. Now, exterminated as unfit for conservation, the wild dog no longer exists in Uganda's national parks — 'too ruthless and too horrible' to be preserved.

One single factor lies behind so extraordinary an attitude: the wild dog's efficiency as a predator. Seldom touching carrion, it relies on its own kills. Understandably, its ravages amongst sheep and goats turn every stockman's hand against it. Conservationists held that if it was not wiped out, it would exterminate many other species — especially smaller antelope, overlooking the fact that wild dog, and the antelope on which they fed, had co-existed for millenniums.

Opposite: Wild dog may not be as aesthetically beautiful as cheetah or leopard but their social life is extremely interesting.

Above: Much play behaviour in wild dog packs seems linked to establishing dominance.

The wild dog hunts begin with a 'meet': one dog arouses itself and starts to hassle the others. With tail raised, it nudges and nips, pulls ears, nuzzles, jumps over recumbent dogs — all the while its teeth bared in a gleaming grin. Such behaviour is contagious. Soon the whole pack is romping about, tails on high. Almost as abruptly as it starts, the meet stops and the pack heads off. Initially there is a little tomfoolery, but now they trot in earnest single file, scanning about them as they go. The grazers on the plains watch their progress with an unease that other predators do not arouse.

When a victim is chosen, the dogs slow down and bunch together, their heads characteristically lowered, ears laid back, tails down and eyes intent as they approach the quarry at a stealthy walk. Tension in the watching antelope now rises. Just as they wheel to flee, the dogs whip up their tails and break into a gallop. In seconds the chase settles down at a fast run of around forty kilometres (twenty-five miles) an hour. One or two dogs, faster than the others, press on the victim's heels to keep it

at maximum pace. The rest spread out behind. When the lead dogs let up, their place is taken by others. If the quarry turns to one side, the pack flankers immediately spurt forward and cut the corner. If the hapless animal veers the other way, the opposite flankers head it off. If the prey has the endurance and runs straight, the chase can go for several kilometres. If, initially, it jinks and turns too much the dogs are upon it that much sooner.

Tearing at the flanks and hindquarters, they break the victim's stride and, its abdomen torn open, viscera pouring out, it is down. Rent this way and that, it dies within seconds. Now the pack gathers round, tails high in excitement, and without fighting or squabbling, tears off the flesh and wolfs it down. To eat a gazelle takes but a few minutes.

Of all the big carnivores, the wild dog seem to follow the most predictable routines. They hunt regularly, both in the early morning and late afternoon and early evening.

In evolutionary terms the African species

of wild dog, *Lycaon pictus*, does not seem closely related to the true dogs — wolves, domestic dogs and jackal. Its nearest relative is probably the Asian hunting dog *Cuon*, but an imperfect fossil record leaves much to speculation. One difference that marks the wild dog out from true dogs is that it has only four toes on each foot.

Social organization is unusual. Many packs have a large number of males — ten out of twelve is not uncommon. Litters tend to be really large, with up to nineteen pups born at once. The mother, however, does not have to suckle them for long; by a month old they are eating meat.

Wild dog were once found in most African habitats other than true forest and real desert. One was seen on top of the 19,340-feet-high Kibo peak of Kilimanjaro, the highest mountain in Africa. It shows how widely the species ranges. Wild dog have a reputation as great wanderers. Packs turn up where they haven't been seen for years, then move on again after a brief stay.

Males and females have separate hierarchies, thus each pack has a dominant female and a dominant male, usually the sole breeding pair.

Wild dog society, however, is still imperfectly understood. Most of the available information comes from observations of packs of about twelve or less, while there are authentic records of packs exceeding sixty individuals. And there are two records — one from nineteenth-century South Africa, one from Kenya by the famous writer Karen Blixen, alias Isak Dinesen — of packs numbering several hundreds. If, on the basis of what is known today, this stretches credulity, it should not be rejected as impossible. Socially, a pack of thirty or sixty would suggest a different order or ranking to that observed in the much smaller packs of the Serengeti-Mara.

Wild dogs have been rare in the Mara for at least two decades. The nearest packs operate to the north around Aitong, on Maasai pastures still well-populated by wildebeest and other antelope.

Above: A wild dog pack tears a gazelle carcass apart within seconds.

Top: Wild dog pack singles out a wildebeest calf.

Above: In panic the mother turns in every direction to chase off the predators.

It's late evening on the African savannah. After a vigorous pre-hunt meet, a wild dog pack sets off at a trot. Soon they find a small group of wildebeest with several young calves. The dogs bunch up and, as a tight mob, head stealthily towards the herd, heads and tails down, ears flat. The wildebeest look on with rising apprehension. At a distance of 150 paces, the dogs whip up their tails like battle pennants and charge the herd. The wildebeest break and run with the dogs hard on their heels. For 600 paces or so the pack press the herd until, slowly, a female with a young calf begins to flag. Now the two are cut out from the rest of the herd and overhauled by two dogs at full pace. These make no attempt to

attack the wildebeest, but concentrate on getting in front of them.

Well ahead, they wheel and face the oncoming victims. The wildebeest stops. The calf stays tucked close to its mother's side. Now the female charges the dogs in front of her. Other members of the pack dash in from the flank and snap at the youngster. Despite a spirited defence, the end is not far off as a dog takes a firm hold on the calf's thigh. Within seconds others tear at its rump and abdomen and it is down.

The mother watches from about thirty metres away as the dogs feed, charges once more and then makes off after the herd.

Top: But the pack converge for the final blow.

Above: The distraught mother briefly returns to protect the corpse.

Flushed by chance, a hare takes off with a wild dog in hot pursuit. In no time others are ranging alongside ready to cut it off — or take advantage of any jinks or change of course. This co-operation between pack members makes wild dogs the most successful of predators. Indeed, they are probably the best hunters in the Serengeti-Mara, with successes running around seventy per cent of hunts started.

But as human populations increase, so do the numbers of domestic dogs — a reservoir for rabies and canine distemper. Theoretically, as wanderers, wild dog come into contact with domestic or feral dogs and

Below: As one wild dog falls back, another takes over as a third cuts off the prey from the side — typical wild dog hunting strategy.

are infected more and more frequently. If this hypothesis is correct it will probably make the species the most 'endangered' of Africa's larger carnivores.

If true, their survival may well depend on radical intervention. In places like the Serengeti-Mara, this could mean inoculating the dogs against distemper and rabies. Whether or not they could ever again be considered truly wild under such a prophylactic regime underscores the region's major ecological message: that the difference between the natural and the unnatural is probably of no consequence where evolution is concerned.

Above: After a quick kill, wild dog enjoy the spoils of the hunt.

Members of a wild dog pack gorge at a kill before returning to the puppies' den to regurgitate part of their meal for the young to eat. This system reduces dependence on the mother to a very short time. In at least one recorded instance, when a mother was killed, the all-male survivors of the pack successfully reared her orphaned pups. An adult which is unable to keep up with the hunters can also avail itself of help. By adopting the puppy begging routine of whimpering and nosing at the corner of another adult's mouth, it can induce regurgitation and thus be fed.

Wild dog, like Africa's other large predators, take a wide range of prey. On their own, or in small packs in thick bush, they may subsist off animals as small as rats. Like domestic terriers, they bounce through long grass, stopping every so often to listen for scurrying rodents, pouncing at the source of any sound.

In South Africa's Kruger National Park, impala form just under ninety per cent of victims recorded. On the open Serengeti-Mara plains, Thomson's gazelle are probably the most frequently caught animal, though wildebeest calves figure prominently.

Relatively small themselves — adult dogs weigh about twenty-six kilos (fifty-seven lbs.) on average — they generally kill animals of less than seventy-five kilos (165 lbs.), but through pack hunting can take much larger quarry. The list of recorded wild dog prey includes grass rats, larger cane rats, porcupine, hare, spring hare, wart hog, Thomson's and Grant's gazelle, gerenuk, dik-dik, duiker, oribi, impala, greater and lesser kudu, zebra, reedbuck, hartebeest, wildebeest, ostrich and at least two lion.

Above: Adult members feed wild dog youngsters by regurgitating chunks of meat.

They have been seen attacking a hippo, actually biting it in the chest and legs, chasing elephant and harrying black rhino, though it is unlikely that they could — or were even trying to — kill these pachyderms. Given to rough play with other animals, it was more likely that they were having fun, mobbing and nipping them.

Hyaena are common butts for wild dog fun in both the Serengeti and the Mara. Moving too close to a wild dog kill, they are often roughed up. The dogs will savage and bite an over-eager hyaena. The hyaena of the southern and central Serengeti, which have frequent contact with wild dog, treat them with considerable respect. But at Aitong, north of the Mara, where dogs were new arrivals, upon seeing a kill they would breeze over, confident of displacing the scruffy little canines. Repeatedly, they paid dearly for this confidence and were roughly handled on a number of occasions.

The hostility that generally prevails between the large carnivores includes wild dog. They kill lion and vice versa; and leopard, too. But wild dog do not frequently steal other species' prey. They take carrion rarely, which is fortunate, for it is quite possible that if they did they would have been poisoned into extinction.

Like their cousins, the true dog, African wild dog are a noisy rabble. At a pre-hunt meet or when begging, they whine and make a curious twittering. They yelp when startled and also have a gruff bark. Should a pack become separated, quite common during the chase, they give a series of drawn-out hoots which, though not loud, carry a considerable distance.

Above: All adult wild dog seem genuinely fond of pups and regularly interact with them.

Even if there are several adult females in a pack, usually only the senior of them breeds. If a subordinate bitch produces a litter at the same time, the dominant matriarch will destroy the second litter. But, as we recorded at Aitong, there are exceptions to every rule. In a pack of two females and six males, the dominant female whelped a litter of eight pups and they had only just opened their eyes when the second subordinate female started to check out other dens to have her impending litter. We never expected to see her pups, as we believed that the lead female would kill them shortly after they were born. But this never happened. Some four weeks after the first litter was born, the second bitch gave birth to nine puppies. Both groups were cared for by the rest of the pack and the two bitches attended to their offspring, with both suckling pups at the same time.

The Aitong pack's subsequent fortunes gave insight into why two litters seldom coexist in the same pack. Rearing a large litter puts a substantial burden on a wild dog pack — not the least of which is confining it to a given area during the three months before the pups are mobile enough to follow the nomadic adults. If they are born when there is abundant prey close by,

this may pose no problem and there is no need for the pack to move. But where quarry comes and goes, as in the Serengeti-Mara, it's an obvious advantage to be mobile as soon as possible.

When the first Aitong litter was two-and-a-half months old, the migrating herds moved away from their den area. In a one-litter pack this would have posed no problem, for the first young were now old enough to follow the grazing herds with the adults. In this case, however, the second litter was not yet two months old. But as the adults could not feed seventeen puppies and commute between the den

and the now distant herds they decided to move. Immediately, the smallest pups were in trouble. On the first day the second litter's runt couldn't keep up and although the two females repeatedly endeavoured to keep in touch it was eventually abandoned. In the next two days two more disappeared. The burden that the litter posed for the pack may also have jeopardized the welfare of the first litter, whose members still could not hunt effectively, yet being near full size, required as much food as an adult.

Above: In an unusual and hitherto unseen demonstration of female co-operation, pups of two litters suckle either mother happily.

Opposite top: Wild dog normally finish off kills long before the vultures arrive. In this case a dog defends a kill on which it will no longer feed.

Opposite bottom: Even the mighty lion does its share of vulture-chasing.

Below: A jackal holds vultures at bay for short periods, but when the birds arrive in numbers, it flees.

As carnivores which do not kill, vultures are near the pinnacles of life's shifting pyramids in African ecology. Six species occur in the Serengeti-Mara — Egyptian, hooded, white-headed, Ruppell's griffon, lappet-faced (the largest) and white-backed (the most abundant). All need thermals of warm, rising air on which to soar and circle and thus have to wait until the sun has heated the earth sufficiently to create this aerial turbulence. Consequently, they are late risers, seldom on high before ten o'clock in the morning, remaining perched during dull, cloudy days.

But once airborne they soar for hours on end, scanning the world below for signs of the dead and dying, watching the hunters for signs of action and, when the omens are good, waiting on them. In turn, and as they watch one another, they are followed by numerous eyes below: those of the lion, leopard, hyaena, jackal and, of course, man. For when they sight carrion and descend, their converging courses pinpoint where it is, allowing the scavengers to locate it and join them in a hissing, quarrelling, snapping, disorderly last rite for the departed.

One evening, as dusk fell, we returned to camp. The smell of roasting meat came from the staff quarters. We asked our men for the reason. They had seen some vultures landing nearby. When they investigated, they found a cheetah on an impala kill. Out came their knives. The cheetah was chased off and the four legs were removed.

Our staff had behaved precisely as lion, leopard, hyaena, and jackal, although in this case the cheetah later returned for the rest of the carcass.

Above: Hyaena and vultures have well-established relationships. When hyaena gather around a kill, the other scavenger waits its turn. This over-eager vulture gets a menacing reminder of plains hierarchy.

Hyaena

Above: Hyaena clans are territorial and, as such, are alert at kills when their riotous feeding could attract neighbouring clans.

Previous pages: Snarling hyaena subdues another.

It is difficult to distinguish male hyaena from females. So closely do the female organs 'mimic' the male's that, other than with mature females, it is virtually impossible to establish sex by eye. Not surprisingly, it was widely believed that hyaena were hermaphrodites.

Not until the 1960s, when Hans Kruuk, a Dutch biologist, studied the spotted hyaena in the Serengeti and Ngorongoro Crater were the veils of ignorance and mystery drawn aside from the species' basic biology. Many seeing hyaena wonder if they are 'dogs' or 'cats'. They are not closely related to either. Indeed, their nearest relatives are probably the viverrids — mongooses and genets, both having descended from a distant common stock.

But hyaena are unusual in that the females are larger and socially dominant.

Above: Hyaena have the most powerful jaws of any predator. They crunch through the skull of most prey right down to the horns.

They live in clans with well-defined territories vigorously defended against outsiders. Within each clan, there are strong female hierarchies in which each she-hyaena knows its place. Recent research suggests that males within the clan are also ordered into a distinct ranking. But they remain inferior to the females. Scattered about each clan territory are a number of communal dens; usually a warren of tunnels extended and expanded from a single aardvark burrow.

Man has long held hyaena to be evil because of their association with death. In times past, these ultimate scavengers must have attended many a human battlefield to feast off the slain. Even now, some Africans lay out their dead and dying to be eaten by hyaena.

Below: Young hyaena listens intently; ever-alert to news of a fresh kill or clan dispute.

Opposite: The hyaena's loping, almost cowed, gait makes them look ineffective hunters. But in fact they are among the most successful predators on the African plains.

Hyaena cubs are born deep underground, in one of the clan's burrows, in litters of up to three. Usually, two or three clan females will give birth at the same time in different parts of the same den. The young are born black with their eyes open, teeth in place. Though they soon walk, the cubs stay in and around the burrow for a long time. For the first eight months they depend entirely on their mother's milk and are not fully weaned until between one year and sixteen months old — the longest dependence on maternal milk of all carnivores.

Cubs may be killed and eaten by adult male hyaena. When following adults on hunts or joining them at kills, the mother frequently places herself between her young and any adult male. Growth is rapid. The black coat starts to turn into the normal spotted patterning in the cub's second month. By one year all that remains of the natal colouring are black 'stockings', which fade in the second year. Full grown at three, it weighs sixty kilos (132 lbs.) but may grow as heavy as eighty-six kilos (190 lbs). Overall, it is bigger than the average leopard.

The spotted hyaena is known best for its call, a characteristic sound of the African night — a drawn-out 'o-ooh-oo' that starts on a low note, rises and falls back to the starting note. The animal's muzzle points towards the ground, not, as might be expected, towards the heavens. It carries great distances and probably notifies other hyaena of an individual's presence.

Even more famous is hyaena laughter — maniacal giggles, shrieks and twitters — both funny and eerie, adding substantially to the species' sinister reputation. These sounds are usually uttered when the hyaena is excited, as at a kill, or during a clan interaction.

Excitement and tension are also signalled by stiffly raised and fluffed-out tails.

Below: Periodically, hyaena cubs are moved from den to den to avoid growing numbers of parasites and menacing predators drawn by the powerful scent.

Now and then, the young of large carnivores have to be moved, perhaps because the litter has been discovered by another predator, or the lair is no longer tenable. In all species the basic technique is the same. Here, illustrated by a lioness and a female hyaena, small cubs are picked up by the scruff of the neck, or the neck itself, and carried off in the mother's mouth. Only one at a time can be carried. Several cubs mean repeated trips.

Do the mothers count? Do they know how many cubs they have? It seems that the 'safety' mechanism to prevent any cub being left out is that the female will keep going backwards and forwards between old and new lairs until there are no cubs left to carry. Once she cannot find a cub to carry, the cycle is broken.

Below: Most predators use the same technique to carry their young.

Above: Giraffe mother lashes out at predatory hyaena.

Previous pages: Hyaena pack gathers around a new-born giraffe, hidden in the grass but still dangerously exposed to the predators.

Twelve hyaena come upon a new-born giraffe, still too weak to raise its head. The hyaena encircle young and mother, twittering and giggling with excitement. Several try stealing forward on their bellies to get at the calf. Each time the mother flails her hooves and drives them back. The hyaena regroup and return, only to be driven off again and again. The young giraffe dies during these protracted attempts, but the mother seems unaware of this.

But now a black-backed jackal sidles up to the dead calf and starts eating. The sight rouses the hyaena even more and their noise attracts other members of the clan. No less than twenty-five eventually con-

front the forlorn mother, breaking her maternal resolve. After a final charge she slowly backs away and leaves.

Before Hans Kruuk's studies it was thought that hyaena were simply scavengers. But his research showed that the species is also an exceptionally capable killer. Like wild dog, a pack of spotted hyaena can run a victim down by sheer speed and stamina. But, unlike wild dog, individuals often take on animals as large as full-grown wildebeest and run them to exhaustion over a course of several kilometres. The killing technique is the same — tearing at hamstrings and abdomen: gory but effective.

Spotted hyaena eat virtually anything. Among the community of predators, they stand head and shoulders above the others in their ability to digest the most unlikely food. They will eat all animals, from insects to elephants. Although there is no record of hyaena killing an adult elephant, strong circumstantial evidence indicates that they preyed on young elephant to a great degree in Uganda's Murchison Falls National Park, south of the Nile. And in their piracy, they do not baulk at trying to drive one or two lion off a kill.

Their scavenging is unequalled. Indeed, they avidly consume other carnivore dung which still has some nutritive value. They can digest bones — even when old and dry — and have enormously powerful jaws, capable of crushing all but the largest. They have been known to devour brooms, shoes and cans.

Given all this, it's hardly surprising that they are accomplished man-eaters.

In Kenya, they probably exceed the toll of human life taken each year by lion. Even in the Serengeti-Mara, where man-eating of any sort is almost unheard of, it would be extremely dangerous to walk abroad after dark, when hyaena are immeasurably bolder than by day.

Above: Distressed mother chases hyaena pack, but there are too many and her youngster is soon overwhelmed.

Previous pages: Mortal combat in the bush between rutting impala stags.

Below: The victor gores the fallen.
Below bottom: Still enraged, it moves the vanquished towards the cliff edge.

Two male impala joust for dominance on a rock ridge. Now one loses its footing and stumbles. Its opponent charges. The fallen animal cannot meet the assault head on. The duellist's horns gouge deep into its flank. *Touché!* The aggressor withdraws a few paces as the wounded impala rises to its feet. It sees the next charge coming, but again fails to take it on its horns. Again, its opponent stabs it in the flank. Down it goes, scrabbling desperately to retain its footing on the loose rock of the steep incline. Before it can rise, however, it receives another charge in the flank. Repeatedly during the next ten minutes, the victor draws back, waits a few seconds, then charges. Each time the long black rapiers thrust deep into the loser's body.

All the while the other members of the bachelor herd snort, roar and cavort, tails held upright — communal behaviour often seen among rutting impala males.

Eventually a charge takes the dying buck to the edge of a rocky ledge. The next tips it over the edge and the maimed body careens down the slope to the base of the ridge. The victor follows, ready to continue its attacks. Now an ever-watchful hyaena enters the stage. Casually sauntering over, it begins feeding off the hindquarters as the victim still gasps for air and the victorious impala turns and walks off.

Below: The mortally-wounded rival falls . . .
Below bottom: . . . where a waiting hyaena
pounces on the unexpected bounty.

Above: Lone hyaena seem to be at the bottom of the predator hierarchy. Even a jackal can send a single hyaena scurrying. For wild dog, hyaena-bashing seems a favourite sport.

Two male lion pass a clump of brush early one morning when one charges inside. There's a cacophony of growls, yells and screeches. The second male tears into the bush. Soon there is silence. Now a lion emerges from the thicket holding a hyaena by the throat. Though it struggles weakly, it is obviously done for. The lion walks a few paces, then shakes the body vigorously for several seconds, walks on and repeats the process. Finally it drops the dead hyaena. Now the second lion picks up the

limp carcass and shakes it with great violence. Then he drops it and both lion stand with their lips drawn back. They walk away, but after a few paces, wheel around, back to the hyaena, and in another paroxysm of rage, seize and shake it again. This happens three times before they finally make off. It's rare for lion to eat hyaena.

The din is heard by other members of the clan, but there's no attempt to rescue their unfortunate companion. After the lion leave, however, the clan comes out of cover

and approaches the carcass. Twittering in a frenzy of excitement they circle it, sniffing. None actually touches it and there is no indication whatsoever that they might eat it. Eventually the vultures plane down.

Hyaena and other predators are deadly enemies. Lion, leopard, cheetah, wild dog, and jackal young are at greater risk from hyaena than any other predator. And hyaena are the most formidable pirates.

Their approach is not a bald-headed rush and challenge, but gradual attrition.

Gathering around the feeding cats, the hyaena gang whoops, twitters and giggles. Scrubby little tails held aloft, they skitter here and there, working themselves into a highly excited state. The more excited, the bolder they become, moving closer and closer, only to rush back and start all over again. Eventually the mob becomes so noisy and threatening that the lion give way.

But lion do sometimes get their revenge.

Above: The relationship between lion and hyaena seems to be one of total hatred.

Above: Vultures skilfully avoid the snapping jaws of a hyaena.

Opposite: Vultures and marabou stork feast on a hyaena carcass.

In short order, the hooked beaks of the scavenger birds dismember the slain predator. Hissing, squabbling, they reduce it to bloodstains and bones. Towards the end they are joined by a marabou stork. With grotesque bald head and dignified mien, this undertaker of the wild saunters over to the edge of the squabblers, his great beak immediately bringing discipline to the unruly who jostle his long, spindly shanks. Now with great accuracy, and long reach, he leans over and snicks a morsel of carrion from the beak of a vulture that has laboriously wrenched it loose.

Largest of the carrion and scavenging

birds, around the turn of the century the marabou was shot to provide downy feathers for women's head-dresses. Taken from the backside of breeding birds, the fashion brought the species to a low state. But the marabous have recovered. They are seen in great numbers in many urban areas — and also about the many tourist lodges that decorate the national parks and game reserves — where garbage is dumped unburned, unconcealed, in the open. They are natural dustmen, often reducing squalid amounts of waste and filth to less harmful proportions.

Jackal

Above: Silver-backed jackal, most common of the Maasai Mara jackal. In the short grass plains of the Serengeti, the golden jackal is the dominant species.

Previous pages: Jackal spies out the land.

'Nobody watching a jackal can fail to be reminded of dogs. Almost every quirk of behaviour, every gesture is familiar. . . . ' So wrote artist and zoologist Jonathan Kingdon. It is likely that the domestic dog evolved from a Eurasian jackal (or a small wolf — which is virtually the same thing). Three species occur in the Serengeti-Mara: golden, a sandy-to-fawn coloured animal with a black tail tip; the side-striped, which looks like the golden with shorter legs and ears, indistinct black and white stripes along its flanks and a distinctive white tip to its tail; and the black-or silver-backed, easily recognizable by the reddish-brown lower body which contrasts strongly with a silvery dark back and black tail tip.

They are unevenly distributed. In the Mara the black-backed is most commonly seen, while on the dry, open Serengeti plains the golden is abundant. The side-striped is seen least of all.

Jackal, which are territorial, mark out their area exactly like domestic dogs. Similarly, disputes and displays occur along the borders or at kills. Their social units seem composed of a male and female, together with young or newly independent offspring. But, just as there are nomadic lion, hyaena and cheetah, some nomadic jackal — principally black-backed — follow seasonal migrations.

As members of a large carnivore community, the Serengeti-Mara jackal interact with their bigger competitors. They fall to aerial predators — martial eagles, and so forth — as well as to lion, hyaena, leopard, cheetah and, probably, wild dog. For their

own part, given the opportunity, jackal steal the young of the others. As efficient scavengers, too, they feed off other kills. Their relative smallness prevents them from driving bigger species off a carcass — except, occasionally, where the timorous cheetah is concerned — and they more commonly share than commit outright piracy. If many lion and hyaena are on a kill, jackal hang about waiting until most have fed. Where there are few, however, they boldly eat off the carcass, at the same time relying on their agility to evade trouble.

In their attention to the hunting tactics of the other predators, jackal also show affinities to domestic dogs. Sometimes it's difficult to believe that they were not involved in the actual hunt. Several times, biologist Eaton saw a jackal run among a herd of gazelle when they were stalked by a cheetah. By turning the gazelle's attention to itself, the jackal's actions ensured success when an attack developed from an altogether different direction.

Afterwards the jackal and its family scavenged the leftovers from the cheetah kill.

Perhaps the behaviour of domestic dogs may rest not so much on clever training by man as on the dog's own innate instincts. In this respect, maybe the domestication of dogs arose when a jackal sought a hunting partner — rather than man having the idea first.

Above: Jackal are generally relaxed in the company of competing predators. Sometimes they even seem to 'chivvy' the larger predators to go hunting — and to make sure there are some leftovers.

Following pages: Kills located near territorial boundaries result in squabbles between different families — and between individuals of the same family.

Above: If a kill is small enough, jackal often move it to cover, away from potential scavengers and fellow predators.

Opposite top: Jackal family investigate remains of a wart hog kill.

Opposite: Hyaena take back wart hog kill from hopeful jackal.

Jackal are not entirely carnivorous. Fruits, such as wild figs, berries and grass, are frequently eaten. In farm areas, they steal soft, unripe maize cobs. Many insects, frogs, lizards, snakes, ground-dwelling birds (including young ostrich), small mammals and the very young of all antelope and other carnivora, are also eaten.

The largest prey is about the size of an adult Thomson's gazelle — animals about twice as heavy as themselves. Jackal families often hunt co-operatively, moving through grass and thicket in an extended line. Prey flushed by one jackal often runs into another. In the kill, jackal again show their dog affinities, tearing at the flanks and, when the opportunity offers, seizing and holding the neck.

In the Serengeti-Mara, jackal diet is dic-tated by the seasons. When wildebeest are calving, they feed on the abundant after-births. They also get a large share of lion and hyaena kills since these predators kill more often at this time and competitiveness slackens.

When the gazelle are giving birth, jackal hunt the new fawns which lie hidden in grass tussocks for the first fortnight of life. This calls for co-operative techniques as the determined charges of the fawn's mother are sufficient defence against a single jackal. If two co-operate, however, one can attract the mother's attention while the other kills the fawn. Some years, jackal live off abundant rodents whose populations are given to cycles when numbers build up to plague proportions and grass-rats scurry everywhere.

Left: Silver-backed jackal grooms young outside the den.

Left bottom: Four jackal cubs await their mother's return.

Opposite: Breakfast time for hungry jackal cubs.

Focal point of jackal family life is the den, usually an abandoned aardvark burrow, in the heart of parental territory. In places such as the Serengeti-Mara, where many larger predators abound, life is no sinecure. While they hunt, they have to keep a perpetual eye open for the bigger hunters that consider them legitimate quarry. Though lion, leopard and cheetah all take jackal, perhaps none offers so great a threat as the spotted hyaena. The others are unlikely to go underground after a jackal. But hyaena breed and live in old aardvark burrows and must take many jackal litters.

We became well-acquainted with a family of black-backed jackal and soon named the family's three cubs: Gutsy, Punk and Gypsy. Gutsy lived up to his name and was by far the boldest of the three, altogether more enterprising. He was first to follow his parents from the den and to initiate games with his brother and sister. Thus it was that on a late evening he lay some thirty metres from the den alongside his parents as Punk and Gypsy gambolled close by the burrow at the base of an ant hill. The quiet was shattered by a screech and fearful commotion where the parents and Gutsy lay. The two cubs vanished underground in a flash. A split second later a martial eagle landed on the low *Acacia* bush next to the den. No sooner was it settled than both adult jackals were at its base, scrabbling and jumping to get at the eagle.

Awed by their performance, it launched itself and flew off with slow wing beats to another *Acacia* some 400 metres distant. The two adult jackal were off after it and again tried frantically to climb the bush and attack the eagle. The commotion was heard by two hyaena who, ever ready to investigate calamity, loped over toward the den. The distraught adult jackal saw them and abandoned the eagle. The hyaena were intercepted and retreated with alacrity, but not before one of them was savagely nipped on the bottom.

Now the two adult jackal returned to where their boldest son had been lying. But Gutsy was dead. The martial eagle had grasped him across the back. Its long talons, driven through his flanks and vitals, killed him instantly. The two parents had been too close, however, for the eagle to make off with its victim.

Caution and timidity are advantages when one is as small as a jackal pup.

Below: Golden jackal are so abundant in Tanzania's Ngorongoro Crater that disputes over kills are common. Then others, like this tawny eagle, take advantage.

Opposite: When feeding, jackal regularly monitor the surrounding areas to make sure that they are not caught unawares.

Cheetah

Above: Cheetah strolls on the Mara plains watched by two nervous Thomson's gazelle.

Previous pages: Cheetah on a favourite lookout point.

Even though it has many species world wide, the cat family is remarkably uniform in 'design'. To the uninitiated, the largest and the smallest are quite obviously cats. Hunting techniques are equally conservative. Most use a stealthy approach to close quarters, followed by a pounce and a swipe of the hooked forepaws. Whether domestic tabby or lion, the principle is the same and differences are largely related to scale.

The cheetah, the odd cat out, appeared several million years ago. Given the generic name *Acinonyx* and the common name cheetah — deriving from the Sanskrit meaning spotted one — its members were all large. Their difference had to do with hunting technique. The stealthy stalk to close quarters was shortened — the rush

and pounce extended. If the single surviving species of today is representative of the others now extinct — and there is no reason to think otherwise — this brought the predator to within fifty metres (160 feet) or so of a victim, and the rush became a high-speed sprint.

Presumably, the system developed in open habitats. There could be little or no advantage in dense cover where the traditional cat technique can hardly be improved upon. The sprint became necessary because open ground made a stalk to close quarters difficult. Such environments are likely to have been arid, typical of the lands in which the gazelles evolved and to which they are supremely adapted. They are the most fleet-footed of the hoofed animals.

Cheetah technique called for certain

modification in basic cat design — a drift towards the dog form of long legs and deep chest; towards a long runner's back and, particularly important, lightness. Loss of weight carried with it a penalty — less muscle and strength. The big 'traditional' cats, lion, leopard and tiger, are immensely powerful, well able to topple animals far bigger than themselves. For speed, however, the cheetah had to sacrifice this attribute — and as it went so, too, did the need for heavily-hooked, very sharp claws. More appropriate were conventional claws that gave a runner purchase on the ground. And these are what evolved with one exception — the dewclaw on the cheetah's wrist didn't touch the ground and remained very hooked and cat-like.

Loss of strength was balanced by a bonus. Seeing the cheetah burst from cover, the victim ran. This built up a need for oxygen. The harder the run, the greater the demand. Breathless and weak after a hard chase, the victim had no strength to struggle — particularly if the killer's grip closed off its windpipe. Death was quick and needed no great strength to inflict. And that is still the technique — a stealthy stalk to within about fifty paces, a charge, a sprint of no more than 600 metres (2,000 feet), a trip in which the still hooked dewclaw drags the runner off-balance, and the tumble. Before the victim regains its feet, it is grasped by the throat and strangled.

Above: Two cheetah cubs make a euphorbia tree their playground. For several days they and their mother hunt in the vicinity of the tree, often climbing into the lower branches to scan the grasslands for potential prey.

Above: When feeding, cheetah are constantly alert.

Different species of cheetah were distributed not only in Africa, but in Europe, Asia and North America as well. Now it exists only in African savannah and possibly in dry areas of Iran and southern Russia.

Cheetah show very little genetic variation, limiting their potential to adapt to new or changing conditions. Animals that exhibit wide genetic variations are best able to: the chances of a novel combination of genes that produce a model able to cope with new circumstances being that much

greater. It seems that some spectacular catastrophe in the distant past may have reduced the world's cheetah to very few individuals and subsequently all modern populations must have arisen from inbreeding amongst those few.

Another area in which the cheetah is at a disadvantage is in competition with other predators. Ill-equipped to compete by force, cheetah survive by giving way. When confronted by other large carnivores, their normal reaction is to bolt. So strong is this inclination that even jackals

and vultures drive cheetah off their kills. When cheetah feed they lift their head at regular intervals and scan the area nervously in case the chase has attracted other predators.

In the Serengeti-Mara, with exceptional numbers of other hunters, cheetah are probably not in the best environment. Food has to be bolted and many kills are stolen from them. More critically, an exceptionally high number of small cubs are found and eaten by their competitors. In seven years study, we found more cheetah outside the Mara Reserve among the Maasai grazing lands, where lion and hyaena were few, than in the sanctuary itself.

All the same, cheetah show considerable variation in what they hunt and eat, and in how they catch it. The prey of choice in the Serengeti-Mara appear to be Thomson's and Grant's gazelle and impala. But their diet is made up of many items ranging from rats to topi, including almost all other antelope of this size, and wart hog, hare and birds.

Above: Barely visible in the Mara's savannah grasslands, a cheetah keeps an open eye.

Previous pages: Female cheetah in high-speed
sprint after a Thomson's gazelle.

Taut and alert, the cheetah approaches its
potential victim directly without any apparent concern for wind direction — which
frequently leads to failure. Initial efforts at
concealment are cursory, though the head
is carried characteristically low. As the
distance closes, so the pace slows to a
careful stalk. Two hundred metres from the
quarry, its stalk becomes distinctly cat-like.
All cover is used to effect and the hunter
pauses whenever the quarry's head is up
and looking about. When it drops to graze,
the stalk continues. The aim is to get as
close to the victim as possible. Now the
only departure from a lion or leopard stalk

is that the cheetah does not hug the ground
quite as closely. The break into the sprint is
usually triggered by the victim. In an in-
stant its head is up and its whole body
poised for flight. As this happens, the
cheetah erupts from cover and within three
or four bounds is approaching its maximum speed of 112 kilometres (seventy
miles) an hour — the fastest land creature
in the world.
 As with most predators, cheetah take
any opportunity that comes their way. If,
during their long daily siestas, a suitable
prey animal should unwittingly come within easy stalking or sprinting range, the

odds are that it will be caught, irrespective of the heat or other disincentive to hunt. Normally, however, hunting takes place in the early morning or late afternoon. It begins as a patrol, the cheetah moving deliberately from one vantage point to another: termite mounds, the lower branches of easily-climbed trees, or rocks jutting out of the grassland. There they scan the surrounding landscape. Suitable sites along the way are scent-marked. The pace is leisurely, but once a prey is sighted, the whole demeanour changes. Like all cats, there's an unmistakable intensity in the stare.

From start to finish the cheetah depends on accurate vision. Hardly surprisingly, then, the cheetah is the most diurnal of cats. It does hunt at night, but not often and only when there is a bright moon. After a moonless night they can usually be found in virtually the same place as they were the evening before. The same is true when a mother has cubs under six months old. She will hardly ever move them at night unless some other predator makes such a move necessary.

Above: At top speed cheetah run at around 112 k.p.h. (70 m.p.h.)

Above: A litter of week-old cheetah cubs. Their eyes will remain closed for another week.

Cheetah are usually born in litters of four or five after a gestation of between ninety and ninety-five days — very similar to the other big cats. The site is usually deep in a thicket. Stemming no doubt from an evolution in open places, there are few records of them choosing caves or burrows as leopard and lion might. The blind cubs, weighing between 150 and 300 grams (five-ten oz.), are an unusual dirty white colour above and black below. This patterning is so distinctly different to the spotted black on yellow coat that develops by three months it is difficult to believe that it does not have some special purpose. But nobody knows what it might be.

The cubs, which open their eyes in their second week, walk by the third week but are kept in a den until they are around five weeks old. The den is changed frequently, the mother carrying her young by the neck. Presumably these frequent moves prevent too strong a scent developing on any one site that might be traced by any keen-nosed

hyaena or jackal. Captive female cheetah have been seen regurgitating meat for cubs in this early phase of life.

From about six weeks, the still extremely vulnerable cubs accompany their mother, and keep close to her. Through a short, low-pitched call the mother can make the young take cover and lie still until she releases them with another call. With this instinctive behaviour she can hide them whilst hunting, and call them to follow her to feed at a kill.

The cubs are half grown by their sixth month and will have been fully weaned in the preceding two months. From then on they take an increasing interest in helping their mother to hunt. Initially, trying to conceal four cubs in the stalk is difficult and much prey is alerted by the inept youngsters. It leads to days of missed opportunities, hunger and discomfort. But during the migration, with many new-born wildebeest calves, food is abundant, despite many hunting failures.

Above: By the end of ten weeks cheetah cubs have survived the most dangerous period of their life.

By the time they are a year old, cheetah are more proficient and can make kills for themselves. The 'trip—swipe' with the dewclaw to throw the prey off balance and then take the neck in a stranglehold needs considerable practice.

The mother helps by catching small prey — such as gazelle fawns — partially strangling them, then letting them go in front of the cubs. We witnessed this repeatedly with the same fawn. The mother kept hard on the cubs' heels to re-catch any prey that showed signs of getting away. From the outset of cubhood, play is frequent and vigorous — an aid to learning control of those body movements that find ultimate expression in the hunt.

At eighteen months, cheetah reach their full stature. Their youth is betrayed by a few wispy strands of mane at the back of their necks and a still somewhat rounded face. But their mother will have conceived again and be ready to give birth. Quite suddenly she leaves them — or they leave her. The young may stay together for a few more months, hunting and sharing their kills. Young females, however, are ready to start breeding from about their twenty-second month. They will already have broken away from their brothers and sisters and gone their solitary way. Henceforth, they avoid other females and only consort with males when the brief mating urge is upon them.

Brothers may stay together in an adult bond and, after a period of roaming, eventually try to establish their own territory. Single males may stay permanent drifters or try to set up a property of their own; an endeavour that is seldom successful except in the short term. More commonly, they join an already established partnership as a third member — a combination that is perhaps the most successful when staking claims to a territory. This will hold until, in time, it is their turn to be ousted, to end their days as outcasts.

As with virtually all cats except lion, adult female cheetah are solitary. Like cats in general, they have territories and effectively seem to avoid one another. The size of territory seems based on the amount of prey and its behaviour. Thus a female might live year-round in about 100 square kilometres (forty square miles). In the Mara there are always enough antelope and other animals to sustain a female and her family. In the Serengeti, however, research by Dr Tim Caro indicates that female territories are extremely large, due in part to lack of stable numbers of prey particularly in the drier south, and the consequent need for female cheetah to move with the migration.

Male cheetah partnerships are considerably more successful at holding territories than solitary cats. Indeed, in the Serengeti,

Caro found that most solitary males were nomads. Territorial males chase them away, sometimes in fatal fights. In the dry south, and central Serengeti, males have to move with their prey, however — though they stay longer than the females, living off resident gazelle when the migrants are elsewhere. In the Mara, males seem to remain throughout the year. Both male and female mark their territories, urinating on prominent objects, scratching and defecating on selected sites. Scent tells other cheetah all about sex, status and reproductive condition.

Cheetah matings are rarely witnessed. Over five years, Caro didn't record one. This suggests that courting and mating is quickly accomplished. So, too, does the rarity with which adult males are seen accompanying adult females.

Above: Cheetah spend most of the day in shade, usually with an open vista in at least one direction.

Above: Cheetah mother watches for potential prey as cubs frolic in the grass.

Previous pages: At six weeks cheetah cubs are probably at their most vulnerable. They have left their lair and now follow their mother. But they are not yet fast enough to escape any large predator.

Play is a fascinating form of behaviour. Most play patterns in predators developed for other purposes.

Cheetah, for example, borrow their pattern from adult behaviour; they stalk, rush, trip, pull each other down, as they would prey. They slap as they would in combat and they assume mating postures.

The main difference between play and adult behaviour lies in the fact that the former lacks the corresponding emotional state.

Above: Cub play often has significant educational value.

Above: Cheetah and her ten-month-old cub survey the plains.

The cheetah is often described as an endangered animal. Indeed, author and scientist Norman Myers warned that the species was little more than a decade from extinction. The same pessimistic view stated that Africa's entire population of cheetah may be fewer than 5,000.

But cheetah are extremely difficult to count. A better idea of their overall status emerges from their general distribution in Africa. They occur widely in Namibia, Botswana, Somalia, Kenya and northern Tanzania, somewhat more sporadically in the northern Transvaal, Zimbabwe, Zambia, Angola, southern Tanzania, Mozambique, Ethiopia, Sudan and several sub-Saharan countries. There is a clear association with dry country. The most continuous cheetah distributions are associated with a crescent about the Kalahari and in the Horn of Africa, the continent's remaining prime gazelle lands. The southern springbok is classed as a gazelle. Historical records suggest that cheetah were once much more common in the far larger Saharan gazelle lands. The apparent rarity of

cheetah is also accompanied by claims that gazelle are now far fewer. The decline of prey may cause a decline in cheetah.

Yet in the closing decades of twentieth century the cheetah is still spread over several hundreds of thousands of square kilometres, split between more than a dozen countries in sub-Saharan, East, Central and Southern Africa.

No doubt, cheetah will decline in overall numbers for a long time to come. Like the other big predators, they compete with man by occasionally taking sheep and goats (cattle raiding is very rare and there appear to be no recorded instances of cheetah killing humans). There will be constant attrition of numbers and range as more and more land is taken for human use. But they are not as easily poisoned as their fellow carnivores and only rarely touch carrion or kills they didn't make themselves. In the long term, their survival will be reduced to two areas: the most arid of the gazelle lands, that man finds difficult to penetrate, and the national park systems.

Above: Male cheetah pairings are common: usually siblings coming together to conquer or maintain a territory.

Among the most common of the viverrid family is the civet. Slow-moving, nocturnal and omnivorous, it is an anomaly in a family that contains the exceptionally agile mongoose and genet. Nonetheless, it is widespread throughout Africa, found in virtually all habitats short of true desert or mountain snow caps.

It eats an extremely wide range of plants and fruits — some of which, e.g. *Strychnos*, are poisonous to other animals — almost all species of insects, spiders, scorpions and centipedes it comes across (again including some that other species of mammals and birds avoid), snakes, lizards, fish, crabs, many small mammals including other lively viverrids, and all forms of carrion. Civet establish regular middens at certain points about their territories and, in the form of pips, bones and sundry fragments, these show just how wide is their range of food.

Defence against other predators seems to rely mainly on bluff. A cornered civet raises its long back hairs until it appears twice its real size. This is accompanied by deep growls and coughs and, *in extremis*, savage bites. Its general silence and tendency to keep to the shadows is equally important to survival.

The civet has been known to man for at least 3,000 years as a source of musk. Secretions from the animal's large anal glands form the base for many luxuriant perfumes. For this purpose civet have long been kept in captivity — particularly in Ethiopia and on the Indian Ocean island of Zanzibar.

A somewhat specialized carnivore of the Serengeti-Mara grasslands is the serval cat. In size bigger than jackal, serval are not in the front rank of the generalized, competitive predators. The longest-legged, relatively, of all the world's cats, it is particularly adapted to grassland. Its long legs and big ears help it to catch rodents. In long grass, sight is not much use — sound is a better guide. In turn this is helped by height, which increases striking range.

Hunting serval stand stock still listening for the faint rustling of a grass rat. Locating a source, it makes a high leap, coming down on the predicted spot — up to two metres away. The rat's subsequent scurrying is followed by lightning stabs of the serval's forepaws, one of which will pin it down until the cat can part the grass stems and seize it in its mouth. The same technique is used to kill small birds and insects.

Occasionally, larger birds such as guinea fowl and even young antelope are taken by a more typically cat-like stalk and pounce. It is notable, however, that the serval's killing technique — holding with the paws and a swift downward bite at the head or neck of the victim — is not particularly effective with larger prey, and the strangling throat grip, so persistent a feature of the bigger felines, does not seem to be used much.

Above: The serval cat has large ears to detect rodents and other prey.

Opposite: Rodents form the majority of serval prey — first held down by the cat's very long legs and then killed with a neck bite.

Previous pages: A civet: common, but seldom seen because it is strictly nocturnal.

*Above: Bat-eared fox are among the most
endearing creatures of the African plains.*

The smallest of the Serengeti-Mara dogs is
the bat-eared fox. Its Latin name — *Octo-
cyon megalotis*, literally meaning 'large-
eared, eared-dog' — while scarcely elegant,
stresses the species' outstanding feature:
its enormous ears.

Like the wild dog, although it is a member of the dog family, the bat-eared fox's
affinities are vague. Perhaps they lie closer
to true fox. Ancestry notwithstanding,
these attractive little animals are highly
specialized. They use their ears primarily to
locate insects, which form the greater part
of their diet. Apparently they can hear the
tiniest movement made by a beetle larva
ten centimetres below ground. Though
termites, beetles, millipedes, and the like
form the vast bulk of their diet, they also eat
vegetable matter and, in a reminder of
more carnivorous origins, catch small
birds, lizards, snakes and frogs when the
opportunity arises.

Essentially animals of well-drained open
grassland, bat-eared fox live in pairs accompanied by their most recent offspring. Life
centres on a den of interconnecting burrows, usually located in an abandoned
termite mound. Their social organization,
however, is flexible and *ménages à trois* are
not unknown, with two females sharing a
male and common den. These fox can
reproduce twice a year, and litters number
up to five. Perhaps this is a necessity, for
they are preyed on by many carnivorous
mammals and several species of eagles.

Harmless to man and mammals larger
than hedgehogs, bat-eared fox cannot survive on developed land. Kingdon has sug-
gested that this is probably due to the
presence of domestic dogs, to which this
species is particularly vulnerable.

Above: Young fox stay close to den and are most likely to be seen around sunrise and sunset.

Left: Nocturnal predators, bat-eared fox start their hunting forays after sunset.

Shadows in the Grass: Wildlife Photography

Good wildlife photography blends composition with sophisticated technology. A photograph is a moment in time — a fraction of a second recorded forever. Photography creates an intimacy with animals that no hunter enjoys. The best thing about wildlife photography is that it invites us all to try it.

On the one hand it is thus very personal, both in conception and perception. On the other, tomes have been written on the physics and chemistry that underlie photographic technique.

But the great problem is that wild animals will not sit and pose. And what the photographic image does not reveal is the endless stalking, the years of study and legions of startled animals that shape the technique of a good wildlife photographer. It also leaves out an insight into animal behaviour and needs — of the terrible realization that habitat is disappearing and that too little is being done to save what remains.

And the field is further complicated by changes in tastes and fashions — as perhaps with all art. Twenty years ago wildlife photographs leant heavily towards documentary excellence — the *National Geographic* style — with perfect focus and front-lighting at a high premium. Today there is a tendency towards 'moodiness' and impressionism using previously unacceptable lighting effects. Our comments on this whole field are made with reservation and emphasize what we have done to get the photographs that appear in this book.

There is so much good equipment on the market today that there's little point in comparing one make of camera with another. Most will have long ago made up their minds about what best suits them. To generalize, the most widely-used cameras are 35-mm. single-lens reflex models with interchangeable lenses. They give through-the-lens viewing so that you see exactly what the camera is seeing. Sophisticated built-in light meters, now standard on most models, save a great deal of time and set the shutter speed without you taking your eye off the subject. Our personal choice consists of a range of Nikon bodies.

There are many accessories for the wildlife photographer, none more valuable than the variety of lenses now available. Indeed, if cost is anything to go by, they are more important than the camera body. From our experience, a 600-mm. telephoto lens is the practical upper limit for field work. Even so, it is difficult to hand-hold and needs a very steady mount. We usually bed ours on small sandbags which we carry for the purpose. Our favourite lens is a 300-mm. f 2.8 Nikor, which, contrary to expert advice, we keep attached to the camera most of the time. Many of the photographs in this book were taken with an 80-200-mm. f 4.5 Nikor.

For action sequences, we rely on motor drives. The chain of rapid exposures greatly increases your chance of capturing the most impressive moment. We think it is essential. Another item we always carry — even though considered obsolete by some — is a light meter. We regularly test the built-in meters against the reading of our Soligor spot meter. Too many unique pictures have been

Previous pages: Wary lion investigates a remote-controlled camera mounted on a remote-control, battery-powered toy jeep.

spoiled by bad exposure for us to rely on auto-meters.

Medium-fast film (200-400 ASA) is probably a good choice for the average amateur photographer on an African safari. For this book we have used the standard Kodachrome 64 ASA film. (The professional version has less shelf life and is more affected by heat exposure.) Since the introduction of the Kodachrome 200 ASA film — which is a professional film — we have used it extensively and are very pleased with its results and reproduction quality.

Most approaches to Africa's big game, particularly in the national parks, are restricted to motor vehicles. In most parks and reserves visitors are not allowed out of their cars to go after game on foot — a welcome exception being the Mana Pools National Park, Zimbabwe. This is a severe limitation. It makes your choice of vehicle critical to your success. It should have good cross-country performance — that is, four-wheel drive and good ground clearance. Do remember, however, that off-road driving is also forbidden in some national parks, so make sure you know the local restrictions before you set off.

Your vehicle should be roomy enough to lay out your cameras and equipment and still allow you room to move easily from one side to the other. Ideally, it should have a large roof hatch for photography in any direction. The windows should be as large as possible, preferably the wind-down variety. The vehicle should be a drab colour. It is much easier to approach animals in a car of neutral colour.

Living in Kenya and being familiar with the game areas, we prefer to drive ourselves. Indeed, we couldn't achieve our results without complete control over our vehicle. But visitors from overseas might prefer to take on a professional driver, knowledgeable about local conditions, animals, and cross-country driving.

National park roads are rough and, in dry weather, very dusty. In this respect, the worst in Kenya is Amboseli National Park. You'll find that the fine, alkaline volcanic dust works its way into each and every crevice of your camera's working parts, so always carry your camera and equipment in well-padded, dust-proof cases. Since this may not be ideal when you want to keep the camera at the constant ready, an alternative is a clean pillowcase with a wide opening. Kept wrapped inside this pillowcase on your lap, your camera is both accessible and well protected.

Many professionals weld elaborate camera mountings to their field vehicles, but we have not found it necessary. Instead, we use a Bushnell telescope window mount, fitted with a standard movable tripod head. The rubber-padded mount tightens onto window panes which can be raised and lowered with the normal winding mechanism to adjust the camera to the photographer's own liking. It is *not* as steady as a conventional camera mount, but it works.

As with any equipment, understanding it, being familiar with it and knowing how to operate it, improves results. Early in our wildlife photography we were much too slow and missed many good opportunities. Speed only came about through practice. We know of no better way to develop the eye-hand co-ordination necessary for good wildlife action photography than following — and keeping in focus — flying birds. You can do this at home in the back yard without film.

Where a long chase is anticipated and the vehicle may not be able to keep up, we use a follow-focusing Novoflex lens with a special pistol grip. This controls focus through a piston movement countered by a return spring. With a 400-mm. f 5.6 Novoflex lens, fitted with connecting rings onto our 35-mm. cameras, we have taken most of the running cheetah and wild dog pictures in this book. It is far easier than the normal arrangement of turning a ring.

Visitors from temperate zones should beware of two factors in the tropics. The midday sun is overhead throughout the year and on clear days produces inky shadows. This lack of fill-in makes for dull pictures. The best light occurs from 6.30 a.m. to 10.30 a.m. and again from 3.30 to 6.30 p.m. At first, we were repeatedly caught out by the speed of both dawn and dusk in the tropics. Light intensities change so fast at the beginning and end of the day that frequent reference to a light meter will save many disappointments.

Good wildlife photography calls for familiarity with animals and it is no coincidence that the world's best wildlife photographers are invariably good naturalists. They know their animals and have a feel for what they are going to do. To the uninitiated, they will spend hours close to their subject in apparent unpreparedness. Then, for no apparent reason, they become alert and ready themselves. Soon the animals start to 'act'; to do things that are photographically interesting. But when questioned about what alerted them, the professional is often at a loss to answer. Instinctive understanding of the animals' general behaviour and biology is what helps predict events.

Our first concerted efforts were directed at cheetah in the Mara. Staying with them day in and day out, we gradually learned their routines — and they ours. The process is time-consuming. There are no short cuts. As important as our getting to know their behaviour was their familiarity with us and our vehicle. And we have no doubt that all the big predators — and probably all the other Serengeti-Mara mammals, birds and reptiles — in time do get to recognize a certain type of vehicle. Once accustomed to your presence they act normally.

Among the most important 'good manners' where animals are concerned is a correct approach. Do not drive straight at an animal — come up to it at an angle or even drive around it at a distance, gradually closing the circle. The watching animal will be reassured that no harm is intended — and you can also watch the animal for signs of stress, rising alertness or alarm. If you sense a negative reaction to your approach, stop and allow time before trying to get closer.

A good illustration of what to do and what not to do came from a recent experience in the Serengeti. Two male cheetah, rather wild and unaccustomed to

vehicles, needed to be immobilized for research reasons. We approached them gradually, an inch at a time, by a circular route. Eventually we were within darting range — about ten paces. We waited a while to accustom them to our presence. Suddenly both leapt to their feet and ran off at high speed — three tourist buses were rushing straight at us. Though still more than 200 metres distant, their direct approach was threatening to the cheetah.

While predators are abundant in the Serengeti-Mara, compared to herbivores they are few. Locating them can be time-consuming and tedious. Short cuts can be taken by watching the herbivores, for they have reason to keep an eye open and there are far more of them than human observers. If they have a predator in sight all heads will be up and staring in that direction. As long as they can see the carnivore, they are not particularly afraid. It is common to see herds of gazelle, impala or wildebeest standing and watching or following lion or any of the other big meat-eaters walking within a few paces of them. They will be alert, but not in flight. When the migration is 'in' and the whole landscape densely scattered with wildebeest, try investigating odd blank spots in their distribution: they usually contain a predator. Vultures, too, are good indicators of a recent kill, as are other scavengers like hyaena.

Initially, and when new to an area, there is little you can do but drive around, watching for such clues and hoping to come across an interesting incident by chance. But with time you'll get to know both the general lie of the land and, more important, which areas particular animals prefer.

We always get our best results from photographing animals we recognize. We get to know their routines, they get to know us, and we can find them with some degree of certainty. Furthermore, we get to know their particular idiosyncrasies and when a certain action on their part signals something worth watching.

Before you reach this stage, however, or if you only have a short time to spend in one area, there are various ways to help you locate animals.

Hyaena do not 'jog' for the sake of exercise. Should you notice one or two loping off across the plains, follow. They are likely to be heading for a fresh kill, or may have heard of a border dispute with a neighbouring clan.

In either case, it will be interesting: hyaena at a kill are an awesome sight. If you keep your camera focused on the centre of activity you are likely to be ready for the shot where the subordinate animal is told off by one of higher rank. The consequence will be a great deal of snapping at each other accompanied by considerable noise.

When a hyaena den is located, it is worth going back at about 5.30 to 6.00 p.m. and spending some time nearby. The young ones are likely to disappear underground at the first sight of you, but if the mother stays at her spot near the entrance, they will soon re-emerge, and within a short time will probably accept you. If the mother slopes off, however, you may be in for a long wait. Sleepy hyaena in the late afternoon are much given to stretching and yawning — quite a spectacular display of teeth.

Hyaena are opportunistic killers. You may find that your car disturbs plains game, one of which may stumble across a sleeping hyaena lying in a hole. However sleepy the hyaena, it is unlikely to miss such an opportunity. We have seen several topis killed in the mid-afternoon. If you find a hyaena in a natural, relaxed state, it will be quite likely to follow the movement of your car by rolling on its back from side to side, looking back at the intruder.

When hyaena feed they remain very alert. Every now and then they disperse on signal to survey the area before returning. Quite often, neighbouring prides of lion are attracted by the noise and come to investigate, so keep your eye on the surrounding area.

Then there are the vultures which arrive at the early stages of a kill and sit around waiting, before moving in once the carcass is reduced to scraps.

You should get good head-on shots of their elegant landing approaches. Keep your lens focused on the centre of activity and your finger on the shutter and you may well catch a shot of a hyaena jumping and yapping at the invading bird.

Opposite: Natural back-lighting adds mood and detail, giving a completely different impression to that of a convential front-lit portrait.

To some frustrated photographers, lion may seem permanently asleep. Indeed, George Schaller, in a study of two nomadic males, found they rested right through from 8 a.m. to 4.30 p.m., their peak activity being either before dawn or at dusk (from 7 to 9 p.m.), when they stretch, groom themselves and each other, play and rub cheeks. It is also worthwhile trying to find them after a thunderstorm when they are usually very active, shaking the rain out of their coats, grooming and playing. You can usually locate them at dusk from earlier sightings; in the early morning it may be more difficult, however, as they often move considerable distances at night. The best way to find them is to listen for their roars, or to note the reactions of potential prey: topis, among the most alert of the plains game, take up a very erect stance once they spot a predator.

Lion and hyaena, which scavenge, follow vultures that fly straight and level and appear to know where they are going, provided the bird does not go too far. The knowledgeable photographer should do the same.

Lion feeding on a heavy carcass often find it hard to drag to the nearest bush cover. They may manage to keep the vultures at bay for a while, but in the heat of

Above: One cheetah mother saw no danger in her two cubs playing around — and on top — of our car. In this case I was trying to get a low-level shot of one cub, while the other stalked me from behind.

Above: The typical results of such a ground-level shot.

the day, the lion are ready to retreat to the shade of a tree or bushes. Now the vultures move in. The lion react predictably and come back to chase the vultures off their meal. This situation obviously presents lion with a real conflict of interest. But for the photographer it's ideal — chasing vultures might go on for several hours and presents prime sequences for action photography.

When you locate a lioness together with one or more males, with one of the males positioned close to the female, you have most probably found a mating pair. Lion-mating represents some of the most predictable and rewarding predator behaviour for any wildlife photographer. You might find, however, that one of the pair is more inclined to mate than the other (when the female's oestrous period is just beginning she often refuses the male, although he will follow in a very persistant manner). Once mating has started, it will be solicited by either the male or female. They will take breaks of about fifteen minutes after which they will start the action-packed performance again.

If you encounter more lion on the move, you are very likely to be able to observe territory marking, which generally takes two forms. The lion approaches either a bush or small tree, sniffs at the covers for a few seconds, then briefly rubs his head through them before moving his body so as to bring his rear close to them. Then, with his tail held high, he projects urine in a series of powerful sprays. To capture this on film will probably require a position with back-lighting. The lion may alternatively squirt urine on his hind feet and scrape them in turn on the ground. After sniffing urine and other scent marks, or wounds, oestrous lioness, ostrich eggs, and so on, a lion will often grimace by opening its teeth, raising its muzzle and its nose.

On two occasions lion tore our toilet tent down. The five young males in question must have decided that somebody had dared to mark their territory — and since the corresponding smells were coming from a funny green structure they decided to have a close look at it.

Many lion kills are made just before dark, and feeding can often be observed by first light next day. Depending upon how hungry the lion are, it can be associated with a lot of squabbling and swatting. (Indeed, whole prides have been immobilized while feeding — every time a drugged dart struck, the lion assumed it had been nipped by its neighbour and swatted the poor animal.) At these kills, keep your camera focused on the action using the highest shutter speed possible and keep your finger on the trigger: fighting breaks out without warning, and is over within seconds.

The cheetah, the most diurnal of all predators, is probably the easiest to photograph in action. It hunts mainly between 7.30 and 8.30 a.m. and in the early evening, at around 5.00 p.m. Cheetah, however, also hunt regularly during the hottest part of the day, when they take advantage of the fact that most prey animals are less alert. if you locate a cheetah mother during or after the morning hunting period, it's worth returning to the same area in the early evening. You may find cheetah cubs at play before the mother sets out for the evening hunt.

It pays to establish how approachable an individual animal is. Do not push it too far, or its hunting will be disturbed. Always keep a respectable distance as soon as the cat starts a move of its own. Driving in front of it and watching it diverge to avoid the car or cars is a technique used by many safari drivers, but it spoils the animal's concentration and disrupts its hunting.

When there are many young gazelle on the plains, cheetah often spot them from a long distance and start the chase without warning. The animal is run down while the adults of the herd scatter. In the case of very young gazelle, the cheetah will try to flush out a hidden youngster which has been seen from a distance but is now concealed in some clump of grass or bush. If the cat hunts larger ungulates, a stalk will proceed the chase. The head comes down in line with the back and the slow careful approach begins. At this stage the photographer should make every effort to get out of the way and not spoil the hunt. It will be easy to determine which group or which single animal the predator has targeted, since the stalk takes place in a straight line.

Normally we leave the cat and drive slowly to one side of the intended victim. We station the car some hundred metres away and then try to relocate the cheetah through the binoculars. Once the cheetah has approached to between thirty and fifty metres, the chase will start. The cat often picks the smallest animal in a group, and you can take a gamble and keep the camera on a possible prey animal. The chase will zig-zag and will often continue for several hundred metres, so there is a good chance at some stage that the action will come within range of your lens. To try to follow a cheetah chase by car and take pictures at the same time is impossible. It will almost certainly result in bruises and damaged camera equipment.

Generally, once the animal is brought down, there is ample time to approach it slowly and get a shot of the cat suffocating its prey. Depending on the length of the chase and the prey's state of exhaustion, suffocation takes between one and five minutes. Again, many drivers decide to take advantage of the cat's committed position and approach closely. This is generally tolerated as long as the cars do not actually surround the predator, a rule which should be observed under any circumstances anyway. Remember, a cheetah chase and kill does not often go unnoticed and other predators may decide to investigate. Since the cheetah is only just above the jackal in the hierarchy of predators, lion, hyaena and leopard regularly move in to take away a cheetah kill.

In one instance we watched a cheetah mother and cub devouring a Thomson's gazelle. We were parked some fifty metres away when we were spotted by some drivers who immediately surrounded the two cats. Somewhat upset by the abrupt intrusion, we started scanning the area with our binoculars. From a nearby ridge a leopard was cautiously approaching the area where she anticipated an easy meal, but the tourist cars and their occupants formed an effective barrier between the

two predators. While we were cursing in our car, the leopard crouched in a nearby bush. Getting shots of a leopard interacting with a cheetah was a once-in-a-lifetime chance.

We prayed that the tourists might go home for breakfast, but no such luck; they stayed until the cheetah had finished their meal. But once the cars started moving off, following the two cats, the leopard dashed out of the bushes, grabbed the remains of the gazelle and dragged it back under some cover. The lesson: even if a cheetah allows you to come close while feeding, keep your distance and you may get shots you never expected.

Young cheetah manifest the instinctive behaviour of stalking and chasing prey. It appears, however, that the killing of prey is taught, and mothers with youngsters often catch smaller prey without dispatching it. The prey normally appears to be in shock while the young animals practise their killing behaviour. Again the close presence of cars might be interpreted as a threat by the mother; and she will kill the animal quickly and drag it to a safer spot to share it with her cubs. Being able to anticipate such a teaching lesson is therefore a prerequisite to

Above: The editors refused to believe this story until they saw this picture.

recording this aspect of cheetah behaviour.

Next to hunting shots, photographers seem to get most satisfaction out of observing and photographing playing youngsters. In cheetah families with more than one young, the siblings will often practise stalking, chasing, tripping and even mating. Resting, during the day, they are likely to lie in the shade of a bush or tree when lighting conditions can often be dull. We have never used fill-in flash, but we know photographers who do with good results, and apparently the animals tolerate it.

In cheetah society, the male marks his territory usually by standing with tail up and facing 180 degrees away from the object to be marked — a tree, rock, or stump. The hind legs are raised and lowered alternatively four or five times during the emission of two to six jets of urine. Again, to catch this on film requires a back-lit situation.

Cheetah, like all cats, pay attention to cleanliness and groups of cheetah will go through what seems like an elaborate face-licking ceremony, where several animals lick each other simultaneously. Pictures of cheetah licking and cleaning each other illustrate much of the predator's appeal.

Unlike leopard, cheetah are not adept at climbing trees, but they do frequently make their way up the more easily climbable ones. The alert photographer can go ahead and choose an appropriate position for the shot of a cheetah on the look-out.

Under the best of circumstances, locating the most nocturnal of predators, the leopard, is difficult. Perhaps the best illustration of how getting to know an individual animal can pay off is the story of the she-leopard on Rhino Ridge. Leopard are secretive and shy, and do not often allow vehicles to approach closely, so in the normal course of events getting a good leopard shot is very much a matter of luck. In the whole of the Mara there are probably no more than six leopard tame enough to allow cars to approach them.

This is all the more frustrating when you know the species is fairly common. At night, individuals regularly pass through our camp on the Talek river, moving between the tents and even climbing onto the roof of the camp manager's house. So it is a particular bonus to make the acquaintance of a 'tame' leopard.

We first saw the she-leopard of Rhino Ridge in 1981. She was young and had probably been born on or near the ridge. In 1985 tour drivers started reporting a very tame leopardess with three small cubs from Rhino Ridge. We soon established that this was the same animal — leopard spots are as individual as human fingerprints. She was unusually amenable, and in the following months we got to know her and her cubs well; she became even tamer in the process, and was then made the subject of a BBC-TV documentary. Initially it seems that this particular leopardess was tamer than most — an individual quirk — but other factors helped. Rhino Ridge and the land about it has little thicket or cover; most trees and shrubs were eliminated by elephant or fire some time ago. So while we could spot her fairly easily, she, of course, could also easily spot us in advance — and the rocky terrain made it very difficult for cars to stray off the road, and much of the ridge was impassable. In effect this enabled her to get away from game viewers who became too pressing, and she had a 'see-through' safety zone.

We were helped in getting to know her by the fact that she had to return regularly to her small cubs. The lair was in a rocky outcrop that had a scattering of thicket and a few short trees. If she was at home this was usually apparent. If she was away hunting, the cubs stayed silent. We would then go and look for her. Our standard technique was to drive around her territory looking for a kill cached in one of the area's few trees. This paucity of trees made the search straightforward. It was also enhanced by the presence of a hyaena clan who shared the area and took a keen interest in the she-leopard's hunting progress. To avoid their attentions she had to get her kills up trees fairly quickly. The greater our experience with this particular leopard the more predictable she became and the better our photographic results.

We learned to read her intentions. As we found with cheetah, when hunting she would go from vantage point to vantage point — ant hills and the like — to spy out the ground ahead. Like cheetah and lion, she was apparently unaware of the role that wind played in hunting success. On several occasions, she stalked Thomson's gazelle or impala downwind and, even though she was invisible to them, they were alerted to her approach.

Our experience has enhanced our ability to read leopard signs elsewhere. Where once we looked into tree canopies searching for a spotted skin, now we look through a tree canopy against the light. The leopard's form breaks the latticework of twigs and branches against the bright sky and is far more revealing. So, too, is the long tail which hangs down in a manner totally at odds with the surrounding branches.

Kills in trees now stand out as they never did before and if they still have some red meat left there is a high chance that the owner will return and offer a photographic opportunity. All these pointers now seem obvious, but it took a long relationship with a particular individual to bring them into sharp focus.

As with all artistic endeavour, we have tried to introduce some originality into our photography. We sought to go beyond the routine approach of taking good pictures out of car windows. Reading others' results, we find ourselves continually asking, 'How did he or she achieve this or that effect?' We found ourselves gradually turning from the front-lit, perfect light shots to creating back-lit and silhouette effects. Many photographs in East African national parks are obviously taken from the same approximate height — i.e., a vehicle window.

To break this stereotype we tried taking pictures from lower angles. Leaning out of windows and using extended eyepieces went some way towards what we wanted, but was not really satisfactory. Again, familiarity with a particular group of animals paid dividends. Some of the cheetah with which we had become very familiar lived outside the Mara, where you can leave your vehicle, and we found that it was possible to lie on the ground next to or under the vehicle and get a new and interesting angle. The animals in question did not seem to be disturbed as long as the silhouette of the vehicle was unbroken.

Intensely curious to start with, the animals, on the whole, behaved as expected. As mutual confidence developed, we found that we could crawl away from the car right among the cheetah.

One unusual instance was getting out of an open Land Rover to photograph two young cheetahs that had got into it.

As yet, we have not tried to touch. Approaching beyond a certain limit usually provoked a warning hiss. Such close contact with wild animals takes enjoyment far beyond the satisfaction of good photography.

We have also enjoyed close contact with wild dog. This came about purely by chance in an altogether unplanned encounter in the Serengeti. We had gone there specifically to get wild dog pictures and, contrary to the pundits' belief that no such large packs remained, we came across a group of thirty-nine, finishing the remains of a Thomson's gazelle just after dawn. A mob of hyaena surrounded them though there was precious little left to scavenge, other than a few large bones. In high spirits, the dogs decided to tease the hyaena.

Selecting one at a time, they would surround it then take turns to dash in and nip its backside. Clearly the victims saw no play in the process and, tucking in their rear ends, growled ferociously, whirling this way and that to face their tormentors. There was a warren of old aardvark holes nearby — possibly used as a den by the hyaena — and eventually driven to desperation, a teased hyaena broke through the cordon and rushed to the holes. Reaching them it wheeled around and placed its vulnerable rear underground. The dogs stopped, went back and picked on another victim.

It was clear that the whole performance was a game. There was none of the implacable hostility that is so fearsome an aspect of how lion treat cheetah or leopard. Outnumbering their victims and taking them one by one, the dogs could easily have killed the hyaena. And from the hyaena's reactions, it was apparent that they had probably experienced this treatment before and knew how to stop it.

Tiring of the game, but still full of life, the dogs set off across the plain. Instead of moving in the single file adopted by the smaller packs north of the Mara, they spread out line abreast over a distance of nearly a kilometre (over half a mile). It was soon apparent that this was a hunting technique, a deliberate drive the like of which we had never heard of or seen before. The area was grassland with clumps of bush and many Thomson's gazelle. Faced with this number on so broad a front, there was no pausing to assess the situation, which is what normally happens when predators hove into sight. Their reaction on seeing the dogs was immediate flight. The dogs, however, showed no interest in the disappearing tommies. They were after their new-born fawns which lay hidden between the grass tussocks.

The dogs went to them unerringly — possibly aided by scent.

In the next half hour or so they flushed five fawns and two hare and caught them all. The victims couldn't outrun the dogs. Any swerve or jink that distanced them from one pursuer put them closer to another. When one was caught it was ripped apart by the dogs closest to the captor and disappeared in a few mouthfuls. The line hardly stopped moving — while dogs at one end disposed of a kill, those at the other were off at a run again. Spread over so wide a front, there was little that we could do to make a photographic record of the technique, so we just followed.

The drive ended after several kilometres when the dogs came across a water-hole. Two still carried small scraps of gazelle that they used in play. Their heads held high, they baited others to chase them — much as domestic dogs. We were surprised by the reactions. Instead of entering a tug of war, the chaser would mount the carrier, even if they were of the same sex, and go through the motions of copulation. The gazelle remains changed owners several times and the game persisted for at least half an hour. By now the day was well on and the dogs went and lay in the water-hole to cool off. It was clear that they had settled for their siesta. If our experience elsewhere was anything to go by, they wouldn't move until the late afternoon. We took up our books and settled back to wait.

For comfort I had put the pillowcase, in which I had been carrying the camera, underneath an arm resting on the door. Unnoticed, it fell to the ground and it wasn't until a dog appeared at the side of the car, grabbed the bag and ran, that I was aware of what happened. I didn't want to lose the bag and without much thought opened the door and stepped out. A dog barked gruffly and all of them jumped to their feet and stared intently at me but didn't run. I slowly approached the thief, who stood watching. When less than five paces separated us, it moved slowly backwards. One of the watchers decided to join in, capered over and seized the bag from the thief and started chewing it; eyes on me all the time. Then more came up to investigate this strange animal; they came from behind to within two paces, their noses outstretched, sniffing.

It was highly unlikely that they had ever been this near to a human before. They were so close that I could smell their body odours and breath. I then retook the initiative and moved forward cautiously in a squatting position towards several dogs who were now playing tug-of-war with the cloth bag. Eventually I was so close that I could seize it. The dogs didn't let go. They kept their holds and for the next ten minutes or so I played a communal game with them — just as though they were domestic animals. Eventually they tired and the bag was recovered.

Heartened by the pack's friendliness, we spread a mattress on the ground alongside the car and settled down for a far more comfortable siesta than originally expected. The dogs lay a little way off and took scant interest in us. The shadows were lengthening when we sat up. The move was a trifle sudden and took the dogs by surprise. There was a warning bark and all were on their feet.

Above: This is no way to photograph game. While it was originally fun it turned out to be very dangerous and most animals reacted to the noise (as they do when hot-air balloons fire their burners).

They relaxed quickly but the rest period was over. They were all well awake and the afternoon pre-hunt meet rituals commenced. Regrettably we were in unfamiliar territory and a long way from base, so we had to leave.

This experience was unique in many ways. It proved that big packs were not necessarily a thing of the past. It illustrated a capacity to play with other species which, while they share it with domestic dogs, is rather unusual. It was really outstanding that they should do so with an unfamiliar species. The way in which they tormented the wretched hyaena, and 'nicked' our camera bag is difficult not to interpret anthropomorphically as showing a strong sense of humour.

We also discovered the reason why, perhaps, predators change their dens as lairs on a regular basis.

When the Aitong wild dog pack moved its den to a new site some fifty metres from the previous one, we decided to use the old burrow as a photographic hide. The idea was that I would sit in the den entrance with my legs sticking down into

the hole. My head and the camera would be just slightly above the mouth of the den. To hide it, we built a canvas structure covered with branches.

One morning after the pack had left for their morning hunt I settled in. I had just found the most comfortable position when there was a crawling sensation along my legs. I tried to brush away whatever it was, but the sensation actually increased. I decided to break cover and investigate.

The sight was not pleasant. My legs were covered with dozens of small, grey ticks, and the mouth of the den was crawling with them — with more and more coming up from the depths below.

Obviously, they had been starving down there and now, suddenly, discovered a warm-blooded creature within reach.

I could not blame the dogs for making the move.

All the same, there are very good reasons why direct contacts, getting out of cars, and so forth should not be attempted — other, perhaps, than by those in close and continuous contact with the animals concerned. The park rules that forbid getting out of vehicles have a sound base. The very nature of lion and

Opposite: Ground-level shot from beneath the safety of a vehicle.

Following pages: Sundown over the Serengeti — day's end for impala on the African plains.

leopard, for instance, invites fatal accidents. They attack their own kin readily, so the risks to a person are extremely high. Nothing makes this point more strongly than the accidents that have taken place with the famous Adamson lion. Commencing with Elsa herself, people have been bitten, mauled and at least one killed by animals that were more thoroughly tame than any in a national park.

At times we ponder just what it is in the Serengeti-Mara that has asserted so firm a grip on us. We take pictures for the same reason that people drew those dream-like bison and elk on the walls of French caves 40,000 years ago, and eland and ostriches on rocks in southern Africa — out of a desire to capture and evoke a feeling that existed fleetingly long ago. No doubt, it's also part of an insatiable human need to collect and own. Perhaps, more than anything else, we take photographs as an entrée, a reason to be in places like the Serengeti-Mara, and to see and feel evolution in motion.

The experience is not always positive. We remember watching a couple of vultures descend by a zebra mare, which moved off reluctantly when we drove up to reveal that she had just given birth to a small foal. As we watched, more vultures came down to await an outcome. The foal was premature, its rubbery white hooves yet too soft for the hard outside world. Whether or not we had come along, it would never have walked. Whether or not we were there, it already belonged to the vultures. So, obeying the rules of not interfering, we drove away — saddened and not at all sure we were doing the right thing. But we never looked back. It is a daily event in the Serengeti-Mara, a stark reminder that life there is far from idyllic.

And there is another paradox. In the Serengeti-Mara, we seek solitude. If someone intrudes on some event, we feel it's a violation of our privacy. Yet we take photographs and advise and persuade people to go to the Serengeti-Mara to experience the impact of the migration, of predators in action, of life in all its raw, uninhibited flow. And we realize this latter impulse is the stronger.

This creates another conflict. The more people who visit these great sanctuaries, the more revenue the host countries earn — and the greater the incentive to conserve the wildlife habitats and national parks. More people, however, also means more pressure on animals and environment alike. And finding the right balance may be the major challenge in administering reserves and parks — such as the Serengeti and the Maasai Mara — in the future.

Acknowledgements

We would like to thank the Governments and wildlife authorities of
Kenya and Tanzania for their help and co-operation.